The BE-Attitudes for Blending Families

Lessons on the Mountain

TERI DOWELL USSERY

WESTBOW°
PRESS
A DIVISION OF THOMAS NELSON
& ZONDERVAN

Scripture taken from the Holy Bible, NEW INTERNATIONAL VERSION®. Copyright © 1973, 1978,
1984 by Biblica, Inc. All rights reserved worldwide. Used by permission. NEW INTERNATIONAL
VERSION® and NIV® are registered trademarks of Biblica, Inc. Use of either trademark for
the offering of goods or services requires the prior written consent of Biblica US, Inc.

Scripture quotations taken from the New American Standard Bible®, Copyright © 1960, 1962, 1963, 1968,
1971, 1972, 1973, 1975, 1977, 1995 by The Lockman Foundation. Used by permission. (www.Lockman.org)

All Scripture quotations in this publications are from The Message. Copyright © by Eugene H. Peterson
1993, 1994, 1995, 1996, 2000, 2001, 2002. Used by permission of NavPress Publishing Group.

WestBow Press books may be ordered through booksellers or by contacting:

WestBow Press
A Division of Thomas Nelson & Zondervan
1663 Liberty Drive
Bloomington, IN 47403
www.westbowpress.com
1 (866) 928-1240

ISBN: 978-1-4908-7396-1 (sc)
ISBN: 978-1-4908-7397-8 (e)

Library of Congress Control Number: 2015904333

Print information available on the last page.

WestBow Press rev. date: 03/26/2015

Contents

Acknowledgments

This study would never have been possible without *being* in a blending family. I am deeply grateful for the experience God has given the seven of us to grow in grace and faith through the years of blending our family.

To Brandon, Brett, Maegan, Lauren and Joshua, who endured the trials and errors of blending our family. Thanks for loving me through all the mistakes I made. Thanks for staying the course as we bumped through the ups and downs. I love each of you more than you know.

To our extended family. You have always been a support for our family in every way. Thank you for your help when we've asked and your silence when we didn't. Thanks for standing by us even when you didn't understand or agree.

To our *family [re]design* donors. Without your vision, prayer support and contributions, this ministry would not be possible. You have encouraged and equipped us in fulfilling the mission God gave us. We will always be grateful for you.

To Ken. What a journey! We have done many, many difficult things over the years of blending our family. But we are still together, still standing firm. Thank you for allowing me to join you on the adventure. I would still say yes. I love you with all my heart.

Preface

We became a blending family almost 20 years ago. It was easy to believe that because we had each been married and were already parents, both of those circumstances would be easy to maneuver. I remember thinking premarital counseling was unnecessary because I had already been married. I knew how to do that. I really was not interested in parenting classes either. Although I was always researching resources to help me be a better parent, I really did not think being a step-parent would be any different than being a "regular" parent. Boy, was I wrong.

When the honeymoon ended and we settled in to the normalcy of life, it became glaringly apparent that being [re]married, raising stepchildren and dealing with an ex-spouse required more than I had. I needed more information, more understanding, more patience, more grace, more forgiveness, more mercy ... I needed more of everything. And I did not know where to go for answers to the million questions I had about how to handle all of the issues I faced.

We looked for books. We looked for Bible studies. We looked for conferences. We longed to have someone who understood to help us as we began the journey. While we did meet some wonderful blending families, I think we all shared the same frustrations. There was nothing we could find to answer our questions. We all just relied on each other's trial and error methods to learn the ropes for blending a family. I knew a lot of families who were blending, but no one seemed to have answers. Only questions, frustrations and failures.

Over the years, we have learned from the school of what not to do. We could write volumes and still never have adequate pages to hold the apologies we owe our children for all the mistakes we made. This Bible study is an effort to help equip other blending families and [re]marriages as they look for answers. God's Word is the authority for all of life's questions and struggles. In its pages we find encouragement and hope. We meet fellow sojourners who teach us how to live victoriously and to successfully avoid pitfalls. We find strength and courage to overcome during the most difficult of days.

The encouragement and teaching in this study is designed to help you and your family live as overcomers. And I hope you will find strength in community by coming together with others who share similar journeys. As you open God's Word and begin to unpack the truths, I trust you will be equipped for the path you are walking. I hope this study will guide you so that you will be empowered as you step into the pages of God's Word. My prayer as that it will only be a beginning for you as you learn and apply God's principles to your journey as a blending family. Trust God's plan for your family and allow Him to do the work of redemption He longs to perform.

May the words you find here be a reminder that joy resides in the heart of the Christ-follower. No matter your circumstance, you can choose joy on the journey.

Introduction

As you are learning how to blend your family, there are many obstacles you face. While marriage is marriage, relationships are relationships and parenting is parenting, when dealing with a blending family, there are many additional nuances, issues, people and obstacles you face in creating a happy, healthy home.

As we begin this study of Jesus' Sermon on the Mount, I hope you will be able to take what He is teaching and apply it to your family. While each family is different, many of the struggles are similar and certainly Christ's teachings are timeless. So as we dive into the study, I hope you will find some new insights, develop some new strategies, and find a renewed hope placing Christ at the center of your blending home and family, trusting that He really does have all you need for success.

I would encourage you to use this study in a variety of ways. First, let it be a personal study for you individually. This is an opportunity for you to dig deeper into God's Word. Wherever you are on your faith-journey, you can always learn new things about God and how He longs to come alongside you each step of the way.

Secondly, I encourage you to use this as a study for you and your spouse. Take time each week to discuss what you are learning as you experience the study individually. Discussing difficult topics is less threatening, when looking through the lens of scripture with its encouragement and truths.

Thirdly, there is likely application you can share with your entire family through family devotionals. Take what you have learned and find ways to apply it to your family's unique circumstance. Use the topics and scripture as an opportunity to engage your entire family as you grow together in God's Word. As our blending family was learning how to come together, our times of family devotional were often a highlight in the midst of relational struggles. You can adapt the material to fit the age(s) of your children and the issues you are dealing with in your family.

Finally, I encourage you to gather with other blending families and experience this study as a group. There is a leader guide in the appendix of this study that will help with discussion questions and additional material for a small group to process. You can gain great insights and encouragement when you realize that you are not alone in the journey. There are others who understand and can share your trials and victories. Everyone will be at a different place on the path. Perhaps there will be older couples who can encourage younger ones. There may be parents who have similar struggles who can share ideas and suggestions for how they have dealt with issues similar to yours. Let this community become a place of help, hope and healing for you and your family. This is a great opportunity for you to build a prayer community as well. When you are in the trenches, struggling, it is important to have others who will stand in the gap, interceding for you.

As you study, you will note icons in the margins. These are indicators for you to stop and read scripture, reflect and answer the prompts given. This is a pause in the study for you to listen to God and personally apply what you are reading. Spend as much time as you need during these moments. Some of the suggestions ask that you talk to your spouse, or discuss things with your family. Enter these times prayerfully and allow God to speak clearly with hope and encouragement.

As you begin, know that God's desire for your home and family is that you experience victory and wholeness. Jesus went about during His earthly ministry healing the people who came to Him. Whether their brokenness was physical, emotional, psychological or relational, He brought healing. Earthly healing was merely a picture of the true, eternal healing. As He cared for the visible, He always spoke to the spiritual need. His purpose and plan was always to bring spiritual healing and wholeness. Remember God has a plan as you begin to process any areas of brokenness in your own life and family. Trust Him to guide you through to healing. While God desires to heal the brokenness of today, His greatest longing is for spiritual healing. Use your spiritual bifocals to see the healing on the surface, but also look beneath and see the healing in your heart and the heart of your family.

You may be wondering what the Sermon on the Mount has to do with the issues in a blending family. Jesus uses this time of teaching to bring some very practical help to people who are trying to figure out how to live. If your blending family is anything like ours', you are looking for answers. You are trying to figure out how to live. While survival may be your only hope, know that God's plan is so much greater than simply surviving. As Jesus reveals God's plan for your lives, you will find very practical application for how to live beyond mere survival. The principles Jesus teaches are meant to equip you to succeed in all areas of life.

As we look at the Sermon in more depth, you will see very relevant application to the issues most, if not all, blending families face. Jesus has answers for the questions we have as we seek to live life as a blending family. Jesus' teaching will help you live beyond survival. He will equip your blending family to live in contentment and joy.

Some of the principles will be difficult. Yet, Jesus teaches that His path is the path to abundance and fulfillment. Trust Him as you walk through this study. Allow Him to do a work in your heart. Allow Him to do a work in your family. Enjoy your study of the Sermon on the Mount. May it mold your perspectives, your attitudes, and your actions as you seek to have the family God desires.

Week One

Lessons on the Mountain

Thank you for joining me on this journey up the mountain. I invite you to relax and listen to the challenging words of healing you will hear over the next eight weeks. As you prepare to embark on this experience, allow God to speak to your heart and bring you, your spouse and your family circumstances into the light of His mercy and grace.

It's interesting that God wants us to learn on the mountainside. There were (and still are) many times along the journey of our blending family, that I've found myself climbing ... and climbing ... and climbing ... what seems like uphill all the way. Sometimes I'm so focused on the climb, that I miss the beauty of the mountain. My aching legs and feet distract me from enjoying the lush green grass beneath them. My eyes are so focused on the path underneath me that I rarely look up to see the beautiful blue sky overhead.

Climbing a mountain is a great metaphor for life. There will be days when the sun beats down, the rocks appear and the wind is still, making the climb difficult. There are also times when the path levels, clouds shade the sun and a gentle breeze cools and refreshes. Sometimes, there is even the chance to sit down in the grass, listen to birds and just enjoy the view.

I don't know where you are as you pick up this study. You may be exhausted with no end to your climb in sight. You may be looking overhead, seeing the dark clouds gather, wondering how you will endure the storm. Perhaps you are sitting by the brook, listening to the soothing water and feeling refreshed as you enjoy the flowers along the bank.

Wherever you are on the mountain, know one thing. God is right beside you. He doesn't leave you alone when the climb becomes difficult. He is by your side, sharing your journey and giving you rest. So come to the mountain with me. Let's join Jesus, His disciples and the crowds. I do believe Jesus has answers for our struggles as we join Him on the mountain.

Who is this man?

They had seen Him around town. He was the son of the carpenter. Yet some had said that He was different. Rumors around the town square whispered that He might even be the Messiah they had heard about from the Rabbis. While He didn't seem to have the demeanor of a Jewish religious leader, He was certainly the topic of many conversations.

Many of the Jews had become discouraged as they awaited the coming King who had been prophesied for centuries. They remembered Daniel's vision of the statue that was completely annihilated by a rock *"cut out, but not by human hands" (Daniel 2:31-35).* The people were looking for a mighty warrior King like David had been. When word began to spread about this Messiah, the people were confused.

He spoke words of gentleness and compassion. He didn't bring the same message as the Jewish leaders. While they demanded that the oppressive letter of the law be followed, this Jesus spoke of living a life of compassion and care for others. He spoke in terms of the heart.

As the story unfolds, we can make some key observations. What is the significance of the plot and characters? When reading scripture, sometimes things like plot and characters can slip by us and we don't realize that there is significance even to the literary elements that we think only apply when we are reading a novel for school. The context of the event often gives us great insights and understanding as the spiritual message unfolds. Before we delve into the message, let's make a few observations.

📖 *Read Matthew 5:1-2.*

Who is speaking?

Who is the audience?

What do you know about the two audiences?

What is the significance of a "two-fold audience"?

What is the location of the unfolding story?

It is important to recognize a couple of things from the beginning. Jesus is speaking to a mixed audience. First, we see that He has called His disciples together to hear what He has to say to them. In the meantime, those who have watched Him and heard Him speak are drawn to Him. Maybe they've seen Him heal and they are curious. Maybe they are intrigued by the unusual nature of His message and want to learn more. The important thing to note is that Jesus and His disciples are joined by a large group of people who are undefined in their spiritual identity.

Perhaps the crowds gathered that day as much out of curiosity as a desire to know this Man. They had heard about Him, and some may have even seen Jesus perform miracles. Some were amazed. Others, intrigued. Some, curious. Others, even cynical. But Jesus came to this place and gathered His newly-called team of twelve together to begin to teach them. But the curious crowds also gathered to hear.

It is also important to note the location of the unfolding story. The plot begins with Jesus sitting on a mountain, teaching. Perhaps there is significance to the locale as Matthew has chosen to set the stage. There is authority in the Jewish mind-set to speaking from a mountain. The idea reminds us of Moses and his revelation from God through the tablets that happened on Mount Sinai (*Exodus 19-20*). Perhaps Matthew wants us to understand that Jesus speaks with authority the revelation that has been given to Him by God.

Also, the attitude of Jesus is significant. Jewish teachers sat in the synagogue when they taught the Old Testament scripture. Matthew is placing Jesus in the same classification as those Jewish leaders who teach God's Word. This connotes more than simply a casual conversation. Jesus is positioned to speak with authority as a Rabbi.

Finally, let's revisit the audience that Matthew describes to better help us understand Jesus' intent as He taught. While the primary audience was His disciples, there was also a crowd. The disciples were His close following ... those in whom He personally invested and spent time with, building within them a deeper understanding of what it meant to BE a disciple. The crowds, however, were largely unidentified in their faith. Some may have been believers in the message Christ shared, but many were not. Jesus intended that His teachings be food for the follower, but a message of hope for those who had not yet accepted the Gospel. But realize the intended recipients of the message were believers.

As we live out our lives, we are called to live in such a way that we are making disciples of Christ as we journey *(Matthew 28:18-20)*. There are those in our lives we are called to spend time and energy investing in. However, there are also those who watch us and hear us and see us living out our lives from afar. They may or may not be Christ-followers, but as they watch us live out our calling, they are impacted and perhaps we will be the example that leads them to faith in Christ. Be aware of your influence. While you have a deep and powerful impact on those with whom you walk most closely, you also have an impact on those who view you from the outside. Understanding the original context of Jesus' teaching will help you better interpret the sermon and make practical application to you, your family and your community of faith.

Today, as we close, ponder your influence. How are you impacting those in your home? Are you discipling the children God has given you? Think about how Christ would want you to lead your family and how He desires for you to care for those in your household.

As a blending family, you not only have the children given to you by birth, but you also have been given the task of helping to disciple children who are not biologically yours but are now family. There are other influences in their lives that you cannot control. However, God has given you a special assignment to help disciple and mold these young lives. As you walk the journey of raising stepchildren, remember God's task for you. He has placed you in their lives in order to be His light and His guide as they grow. Step-parenting is an especially difficult task. Trust God to guide you each step of the way. Be willing to invest in them as God desires. You may only see your stepchildren twice a month, but allow God to use that time to grow them and deepen their faith walk.

Tomorrow, we will begin our journey through the message Christ shared. Spend time in prayer. Ask God to open your heart to the transforming work He longs to do in you, in your marriage and in your family.

Day Two

Understanding the Blessed's

Today we will get a cursory overview of what most people term the Beatitudes from the Sermon on the Mount. Over the coming days and weeks we will dig much deeper into each beatitude, but for today, I want you to just become familiar with Jesus' teaching.

During His earthly ministry, Jesus employed a number of different teaching styles. Some of His teachings came in the form of questions to those within earshot. Understandably, His questions caused the listener to ponder. He often did this when talking to the religious leaders. Another style that characterized His teaching utilized contrasts: "You've heard it said … but I say." You can find this literary style used later in the Sermon on the Mount when Jesus was teaching about the law and grace.

Jesus also used parables masterfully in helping his listener understand deep, sometimes complex spiritual truths. He would tell a story relevant to the context of the listener, allowing profound spiritual truths to be extracted from the simple tale. The Gospels are filled with examples of the parables Jesus told.

But during the section of Jesus' sermon we are looking at today, he spoke proverbially. These few verses would be reminiscent of what theologians would call wisdom literature. The entire book of Proverbs is an example of wisdom literature. Short statements that give a specific, practical application of truth.

Before we begin to dig deeper, I want you to simply make a list of the qualities Jesus shares.

Read Matthew 5:1-11.

Record each of the blessed's.

1.
2.
3.
4.
5.
6.
7.
8.
9.

Now, beside each quality, list the reward for exhibiting that quality.

5

Before we move on, we need to take some time to understand one of the key words of the entire section of scripture. In order to understand the intent of Jesus' message, we must understand the meaning of the word *blessed*.

Sometimes people like to substitute the word "happy" for "blessed." In fact, there are a couple of translations of the Bible that use the word happy. While the intent may be to bring happiness, we often equate happiness with what happens to us. We are happy based on our circumstances. The *blessed's* can be translated happy, but I want you to think in deeper terms going beyond what happens. Allen Ross defines the word *blessed* as follows: "This term is an exclamation of the inner joy and peace that comes with being right with God."[1] While understanding that Jesus is giving a discourse on righteous living, He indicates that in order for one to be truly at peace with God and having inner contentment, the key is living righteously. Remember, Jesus is speaking at a time when the law was the foundation for righteousness. The Jewish leaders had even taken the Law of Moses and added to it in order to assure that "righteousness" was lived out to the very smallest detail. Jesus' teaching will rock the world of the Jews. He will take their adherence to law and try to help them understand that mankind can never earn his righteous standing before a Holy God. Christ Himself will become our righteousness. Our right standing before God comes because we choose to accept the free gift of grace from a loving God. What Jesus teaches in this passage is certainly counter-culture for the time, and a challenge for us to understand even today in light of our human tendencies.

Some have taken the name of this discourse and applied a play on words. In fact the title of this study employs this play on words. The Beatitudes could be viewed as the Be-attitudes. In other words, what are the attitudes that Christ would want us to exhibit as a part of our very nature? How would he desire that we "be"? Jesus is helping His listeners understand that certainly what we do is important, but the transformation happens in our inner being ... who we are on the inside. How we act is a reflection of what Christ has done for us in the very core of our being.

As we end our time together today, I encourage you to spend some time meditating on the scripture, and asking God to open your heart to His Word. One of the things that helps me have a fresh perspective on a well-known verse of scripture, is to read it in another translation. For your remaining study time, I want you to read and meditate on this passage as translated by Eugene Peterson in The Message. Allow your mind and heart to meditate on the *blessed's* you read. Consider what they mean in your own life and ask God to deepen your understanding as you ponder. Ask God to help you begin to understand what it means to live *blessed*.

"When Jesus saw his ministry drawing huge crowds, he climbed a hillside. Those who were apprenticed to him, the committed, climbed with him. Arriving at a quiet place, he sat down and taught his climbing companions. This is what he said:

'You're blessed when you're at the end of your rope. With less of you there is more of God and his rule.

'You're blessed when you feel you've lost what is most dear to you. Only then can you be embraced by the One most dear to you.

'You're blessed when you're content with just who you are—no more, no less. That's the moment you find yourselves proud owners of everything that can't be bought.

'You're blessed when you've worked up a good appetite for God. He's food and drink in the best meal you'll ever eat.

'You're blessed when you care. At the moment of being 'care-full,' you find yourselves cared for.

'You're blessed when you get your inside world—your mind and heart—put right. Then you can see God in the outside world.

'You're blessed when you can show people how to cooperate instead of compete or fight. That's when you discover who you really are, and your place in God's family.

'You're blessed when your commitment to God provokes persecution. The persecution drives you even deeper into God's kingdom.' Matthew 5:1-12 (The Message).

As you have read through these beatitudes, can you choose one that speaks most clearly to the experiences of your blending family today? Record it here.

What would you like to see God do with this beatitude in your family?

What will it take? What is your responsibility in accomplishing this?

Spend some time sharing what you have written with your spouse. Talk about what God is revealing to each of you about your family. What does God want to do in your family?

Close with a time of prayer, seeking God's favor in your life, your marriage and your family.

Day Three

Lessons from the Old Testament

One of my favorite things about scripture is that everything is tied together. Scripture confirms scripture. It is always amazing to me the grand detail of God's complete revelation through scripture. Certainly an assurance that His hand has been on His Word from the beginning. He has orchestrated man's pen to provide clear, consistent teaching that helps us live this life with confidence, knowing that He is guiding us each step of the way. In order to get a better understanding of the beatitudes, let's step back into the Old Testament for a bit.

Read Isaiah 61:1-3.

Record what Isaiah says about the Lord's favor.

In considering this Old Testament passage, we see Jesus revisiting some of the same ideas the prophet Isaiah shared. It is interesting that out of all the Old Testament prophets, Isaiah spends more time discussing the coming Messiah, both as suffering servant and conquering king than any of the other Old Testament prophets. In chapter 4, Luke records Jesus reading this passage in the temple. His audience was a group of Jewish leaders who seemingly could not embrace the Gospel because the law was in their way. Jesus wanted the Jews to understand the coming kingdom, and what it would be like. He also wanted them to understand what it would take for them to enter it.

Jesus came to help us understand that living the Christ-life is about far more than simply following rules or laws. Jesus came to teach us that to live righteously requires a transformation of our heart. As we begin to look at each of the beatitudes, keep in mind that Jesus is talking about our attitudes and motives as much as He is considering our actions.

However, let us never believe that our actions are separate from what is on the inside, in our hearts. True heart-transformation will bring about a transformation in our actions as well. If faith has truly opened our heart to the Holy Spirit, our actions will reflect the change of heart. Further along in Jesus' Sermon on the Mount, He addresses this very concept.

Read Matthew 7:15-20.

What is Jesus warning?

What does He say about their ability to deceive?

What do you think Jesus means when He talks about bearing fruit?

While Jesus is specifically warning against false prophets, the principle can be applied to anyone. Jesus is providing a great analogy of looking at the actions to determine the nature of the heart. While figs are not grown on thistle bushes, so habitual bad actions cannot be the result of a clean heart. When the Holy Spirit moves in and dwells in the heart of the believer, the eventual result will be fruitful actions.

It is important to note that transformation may be a process. Someone who accepts Christ as Savior is immediately filled with the Holy Spirit. However, a true life transformation will likely come over time. Deliverance from habitual sin may be a journey. In fact, often deliverance from anything is a journey rather than an instantaneous event. God has His own timing and His timing is for a reason.

Through the course of my own journey through the illness and death of a spouse, blending a family, and the mountain tops and valleys inherent in any family, I have learned the word deliverance has a different definition than for some. While I do believe that God can immediately deliver someone *out* of their current circumstances (Saul in *Acts 9* is a good example), what He is working in me is deliverance *through* my circumstance.

We often think of deliverance as an instantaneous change. A magical, hocus-pocus transformation. Certainly God can deliver any way He chooses. What I find most often is that transformation is a process. The deliverance from an old way of life happens over time. While we are completely filled with the Holy Spirit at the time of our salvation, learning how to release the power of the Holy Spirit over sin in our life may require consistent spiritual discipline. After all, deliverance through our circumstances allows us to exercise our spiritual trust muscles. We learn how to rely on God and His transforming power each moment of our life.

If you are in a difficult circumstance today, you may be begging God to deliver you out of your circumstance. While He is faithful to deliver you, He also knows what is best for you. Once again, Paul is a great example. He experienced immediate deliverance when He encountered God's Spirit on the road to Damascus. His salvation was immediate and his change in perspective instant. But when he prayed that God deliver him from the thorn in his flesh, God answered that his deliverance would be *through* the thorn. We will look at this experience of Paul's later in our study, but for now let this serve as an illustration that deliverance can be experienced differently.

There may be something in your own life that you long to overcome. God says, "Stay close to Me. I want you to depend on Me to help you through this. Every moment of your life, I want you to know that I am beside you, strengthening you and giving you enough of My grace to make it through. You have My power in you to overcome." The longing of the heart of God is that you trust **Him**. Not His plan or His purpose so much as just trusting Him.

Stay close to Him. Talk to Him. Rely on Him. Depend on Him. Trust Him. If God has truly done a transforming work in you on the inside, eventually your actions will reflect your change of heart.

    If you were to ask God to deliver your marriage or blending family from something today, what would it be?

Are there areas in your marriage and family where God is already at work bringing deliverance?

As you close your study time today, ask God to speak to you about any area where He wants to bring deliverance in your marriage and family.

Day Four

Laying a Foundation

"Blessed are the poor in spirit, for theirs is the kingdom of heaven." Matthew 5:3

Last fall, I had the honor to do something that was a first for me. It was something that surprised those who only knew me casually, and completely astounded those who knew me well. I must confess to being described as a girly-girl. You know. I like to wear dresses. I like to dress up. I mean really dress up. As a little girl, I had a secret desire to be Miss America. I played with dolls instead of balls. I'd rather go to the Symphony than a Cowboys game and I don't like to sleep outside. Get the picture? A girly-girl.

But I digress. Back to last fall. I got to help build a house. That's right. Build. A. House. The whole house. And the other amazing part of the experience was that the entire team, except for an electrician "coach" were women. We worked through Buckner International and the Rio Grande Valley Baptist Association to provide a new home for a family in need on the border in South Texas.

When we arrived at the build-site, the materials were provided and we were ready to begin. But, I noticed that there was already a pier-and-beam foundation in place. The expert builders had given us a place to start. They had laid the foundation upon which the whole house would stand.

As I've spent a number of years commuting to downtown Dallas for work, I've observed the erecting of a number of tall buildings. The amazing part to me, is that the construction crews spend far more time on the hole in the ground and what's underneath that we don't even really see, than they do actually putting the building together. The taller the finished building, the longer they work on the base. As a novice home builder, my take away is that what matters most in ensuring the building's safety and security, lies in what happens with the foundation.

We could say the same thing when we are building our home. Not our physical home, but our relational home. Our family. The foundation is the most important. Once again, Jesus has a word about this later on in His Sermon on the Mount.

🐾 *Read Matthew 7:24-27.*

Notice that Jesus uses the analogy of building a house. He lets His listeners know that storms will come. He does not say *if* the storms come. He talks about *when* the storms come. He tells the people of the importance of building their spiritual house on the rock instead of sand. The rock provides a solid foundation for the home to stand when the storms come, the waters rise, and the winds blow.

Do you want your family to be strong and secure when trouble comes? Jesus says, spend time building a strong foundation. The storms *will* come. In your new family, you will have issues that arise with ex-spouses. You will have problems with stepchildren. You will disagree about finances. You will struggle to build positive communication patterns in your newly-formed family. There will be differences of opinion in parenting. But Jesus said, if you'll build your new family upon Him and His principles for right living, your family will be strong and stable through the storms.

So, what does all this have to do with being poor in spirit? Let's dig a little deeper. Everyone in your new family has come through pain. Everyone in your new family has walked through brokenness. There are relationships that are fractured. Security has been compromised. Trust has been lost. Many, many things have accompanied your family's coming together. You are beginning. But it is different this time, because you are beginning *again*.

As you deal with issues stemming from the past, it is critical that you allow God to take the past. The past cannot be changed. What we choose to do with the past not only impacts our present, but our future as well. In our own strength, we have no power to overcome anything. But understanding that an All-Powerful God can completely bear the weight of our past, gives us the freedom to enjoy the present. Being poor in spirit helps us recognize that we are powerless to stand without the power and presence of God Himself. Let's look more closely at what it really means to be *poor in spirit*.

The passage we looked at in Isaiah doesn't specifically refer to the "poor in spirit," but it does help give meaning to the concept. Isaiah was addressing the exiled Jews who had lost their land and possessions. They were certainly poor by human standards. The underlying message of poverty was more spiritual than physical. The Jews were impoverished spiritually because they were separated from God by their choice to walk in disobedience. God often uses the physical circumstances He allowed for the nation of Israel to act as a picture of their spiritual condition.

In *Luke 4:18*, Jesus enters the synagogue and reads the words of Isaiah to try to help the Jews gathered there understand their spiritual poverty. As He speaks in the Sermon on the Mount he again uses the analogy of poverty to point those listening to recognize their spiritual poverty.

While Isaiah brought hope to the Old Testament Jews that they would someday experience a freedom from their physical oppression, Jesus shared a message of freedom from spiritual oppression. Where Isaiah brought hope for those who desired to return to their homeland, Jesus brought hope to the hurting heart.

🐾 Consider your family. On the scale of hope versus oppression, where would you rate your family?

If you find yourself still feeling oppressed, as a family, what are some things you might consider to help move toward hope?

Are there things from the past that keep your family oppressed? Is so, resolve to look to God and trust Him to bring freedom and hope. Perhaps you and your spouse can spend some time looking at what being *poor in spirit* means in your family.

In the Sermon on the Mount, Jesus teaches that poverty of spirit is a picture of spiritual humility. No one can approach the Kingdom of heaven on their own merit. Mankind is utterly without hope for salvation on their own. Keeping the law or a righteousness of their own will never be enough to open the gates of heaven. We are completely spiritually bankrupt and have no hope of eternal life outside of Christ Himself. Poverty in spirit says that I cannot come to God on my own merit. However, Christ offers a free gift of salvation if I come humbly and repentantly to receive it. My salvation has nothing to do with me and everything to do with Jesus.

This "non-works-based" concept of salvation is counter to the Jewish belief that righteousness is the result of one's ability to keep the law. Jesus teaches that no one can fully keep the law, and the only possibility for eternal salvation is through accepting the gift of grace bought on the cross by Christ Himself.

Are there members of your family who have not yet accepted God's gift of salvation? Pray for them. Ask God to help you share the love of Christ in tangible ways. Pray that God will open their heart to His saving grace.

Note the tense of this beatitude. *"Blessed are the poor in spirit, for theirs **is** the kingdom of heaven"* (emphasis mine). Notice that the kingdom of heaven is present tense. Understanding the need for total dependence on God for everything from eternal salvation, to how to live life allows us to experience God's kingdom *now*. In *John 10:10* Jesus teaches, *"The thief comes only to steal and kill and destroy; I came that they might have life, and might have it abundantly."* Jesus is saying that if we abide in Him, we can experience a fulfilled, contented life. When we live continually experiencing a deep dependence on Him alone, we can have peace and contentment, no matter our life's circumstance.

So how does being poor in spirit impact the way you live your life? Certainly your salvation is dependent on your acceptance of Christ as the way to heaven. But how does this apply to how you live today? Record your thoughts.

Coming to Christ for salvation requires a complete dependence on Him outside of our own ability to save ourselves. This is also an indication of how God desires we live our life as well. Self-sufficiency is a natural, fleshly characteristic. However, to truly live a *blessed* life, Jesus teaches that our dependence upon Him *becomes* our way of life. Self-sufficiency takes our focus off of Him and places it upon ourselves. He longs for us to depend on Him for everything in life.

When it comes to blending a family, being self-sufficient may seem like the best way to manage and control this seemingly out-of-control group of people. After all, you came to this relationship after being single … and probably even being a single parent. *You* were the only person you had to depend on. There was no one else with whom to share the burdens and responsibilities of life. If you didn't do it, it just didn't get done.

However, Jesus is offering you the opportunity to experience His blessing. He said that for those who are poor in spirit, the kingdom of heaven is theirs. How can you let go of the reins of your family, and give them over to Jesus?

It starts with understanding our own inadequacy and being willing to depend on the only One who can truly manage family dynamics. How often do you pray and ask God to take over your home and the people in it? How willing are you to let go of the control and trust Him to direct the relationships and dynamics within your home?

Before you think I'm asking you to just throw up your hands and give up, understand what God wants for you. He isn't asking you to give up. He's asking you to join Him and allow Him to work through you to build the kingdom-of-heaven-on-earth family He desires for you. He desires that your new family come together in love and unity. He desires that you build relationships that both honor Him and bless your family. He longs to be the healer and hope, rebuilder and restorer for your new home.

Can you really do it all by yourself? Can you bring healing to you and your spouse from past hurts? Can you help the children in your household recover from the brokenness of death or divorce and come together to build bonds of love and trust? God may be asking you to release some things to Him. Spend some time in prayer and record anything you believe God may be speaking to you.

As you close your time in the Word, take some time to talk to God and evaluate where you are on the dependency scale. Are you a ten and completely self-sufficient? Or do you find yourself closer to a one, depending totally on God for everything in your life? If most of us are honest, we would probably be somewhere on the high side of the middle. In order to fully depend on God, we must fully trust that God will not let us down. That can be tough for someone who has endured the loss of mate. Whether they died, or we were separated by divorce, we know what it means to be abandoned.

Be honest with God. Tell Him if you are afraid of trusting Him to take care of you and your family. God will be consistent when we are not. Gratefully, God's faithfulness does not depend on us, it depends on Him. And He is always faithful. Spend some time in prayer asking God to give you the courage to depend on Him to bring you and your family into a relationship of total dependence.

Day Five

Being Dependent

In today's world, independence and self-sufficiency are highly valued. We try to teach our children to be independent so they can take care of themselves. Especially in western cultures, we encourage independence. We view dependence as a weakness. When someone can't make it on their own, and must rely on someone else, we nod our heads and mumble to ourselves how grateful we are that we are independent.

But Jesus taught that we are to be completely *dependent*. Not on another human, but on God Himself. Being poor in spirit identifies man's most basic need. His need for salvation. Our eternal destiny cries out for salvation, and our daily walk is heavy and oppressive unless it is lived out in salvation.

The first beatitude itself tells us how important recognizing our poverty in spirit really is. Once we recognize our need for God, we inherit the kingdom of heaven. The most basic lesson of this beatitude is that once we realize we can never achieve righteousness on our own, we can accept God's righteousness through Christ, and the kingdom of heaven becomes ours. One of the greatest illustrations of our dependence on God can be found in *John 10*. Let's take a short visit there to see what God has to say about our need for Him.

Read John 10:1-18.

How does Jesus identify Himself in *John 10:11,14*?

What does the Good Shepherd do for the sheep?

What does *John 10:3-4* say about the Shepherd?

As you read this passage, know that Jesus is the Good Shepherd and we are His sheep. That might not mean much unless you understand about sheep and shepherds. When I did some study on why Jesus would use these animals and this relationship to describe His relationship with us, it was eye-opening.

As I studied, I discovered that sheep are the least intelligent animal on the planet. Sheep have no defense mechanism. They are not bright enough to find food for themselves. They are the ultimate "followers." If one sheep runs over the edge of a cliff, all the other sheep will blindly follow.

Without someone to take care of them, sheep would surely become extinct! But, in steps the shepherd. Interestingly, shepherds don't usually tend their sheep out of obligation. They tend the sheep because of their deep love of the sheep. They view the sheep with a heart of compassion, and will risk their lives to protect the sheep. The shepherd is always alert, watching for the wolves that long to devour the sheep. The shepherd works day and night to find pastures for food and ponds for water. The shepherd's hook will pull the stiff-necked, wayward sheep back into the safety of the fold.

I think the analogy is clear. Not only are we little sheep dependent on God for our eternity, we are also dependent on Him to protect us and feed us and provide for us in ways we never could. God sees the danger ahead. He is able to protect and provide a safe refuge. God knows what we need even before we know we need it. He will provide for all of our needs: physical, spiritual, emotional, relational. God cares for us out of His heart of compassion. He cares for us not out of obligation, but because He loves us.

So what does this mean for you and your family to learn to depend on Him? It all starts with depending on Him for your eternity. Once you are secure in that, you can begin to learn how to depend on Him each day, for every single need you have. Take a few minutes to consider the following questions.

How do you depend on God with your blending family?

What is the goal or your desired outcome?

What is your first step in achieving the goal?

What do you think being *poor in spirit* really looks like in a blending family?

For me, the hardest thing I have ever done was to blend a family. I was completely inadequate when it came to step-parenting, dealing with an ex-spouse and learning how to build a new marriage and family. I had no hope of any kind of contentment, or success or fulfillment without the Holy Spirit. I had to completely depend on His love, grace and compassion for this new family of mine. I had such a limited capacity when it came to caring for these people who were now in my home. I couldn't heal their hurt. I couldn't fill their needs. I became frustrated and impatient with their differences. It was only through intense prayer, and intentionally choosing to let God fill my heart, mind and spirit with Him and Him alone, that I could walk through the early days of blending our family.

As you finish out the week, spend some time in prayer. Listen to God. Ask Him to show you how He wants to work in you. Let Him be in control of your mind and emotions. Look for Him to work a miracle with that one thing that you can't seem to conquer in your blending family. Pray intensely for that one family member who is the most difficult for you. Be willing to completely depend on Him.

You're blessed when you're at the end of your rope. With less of you there is more of God and his rule. Matthew 5:3 (The Message).

Week Two

Managing the Mourning

It felt so surreal. Here I was, a young woman with young boys. I should be getting dressed to attend a PTA meeting at the elementary school, or getting ready to chaperone a field trip. But this Thursday morning as I stood and looked in the mirror, the one who looked back at me was dressed in black. She was trying to look less exhausted and haggard. She wanted to be going anywhere else that day. But the woman who stared back at me from inside that mirror, was me. And I was getting dressed to attend my own husband's funeral.

It really seemed otherworldly at the time. Something I was watching in a tear-jerker chick-flick. But it was none of that. It was real. It was my life.

As I walked through the moments and hours and events of that day, all I could think about was getting into bed that night. I wanted my boys to survive the day. I wanted to survive the day. I wanted us to all go to bed and wake up the next morning with the relief that it had all been nothing but a terrible nightmare.

But the realities of the day became all too clear as a procession of black limousines pulled up to a church full of mourners. It was a January day. Actually, it was my 15th wedding anniversary. But the sky was clear and the sun shone brightly. The air carried a briskness that grabbed the breath, but at the same time was refreshing and invigorating. I think God knew I could never endure this under the oppressive heat of summer.

As I put one foot in front of the other throughout that day, I did so without much feeling. There were so many people to greet and thank and hug. The line at the cemetery seemed endless and I remember wondering why I could no longer feel my feet beneath me.

Finally it was time to travel back to the church for the customary family meal. I don't remember what was served. I don't remember if it tasted good. I don't really even remember if I ate any of it. I felt empty. I didn't feel sad or anxious or depressed. I just didn't feel.

Things had been so busy since my husband had died two days earlier. Much of what we did was pre-planned because he had been sick for so long. But there was still so much to do to prepare. And the people. There were always lots of people everywhere. I don't remember conversations. I don't remember what people said or did. I just remember people.

After lunch, the processional brought everyone back to my house. I remember getting out of the car and going into my house. I stepped in the door and just stood. So many people.

So much food. So many flowers. My house was a-buzz with activity, but I felt completely and totally alone.

My seven and nine year old boys were preoccupied at the time with their cousins. I was glad they were playing and seemed to be having fun. I have since learned that children often deal with their grief by doing what they normally do. I sat on the sofa and heard voices having conversations, but I didn't follow what anyone was saying. It was just noise.

Exhausted family members and friends began preparing to leave. It had been such a long journey and everyone was so tired. My boys were going home with my parents for the weekend. Grandma's house would be a nice distraction.

As I sat listening to all the voices in the room, I suddenly had an overwhelming need to just get out. I needed out of that house. I couldn't breathe. I had to get out. So I changed clothes and left for the mall. That may sound strange, but I longed to do something that a normal 37-year-old woman would do. The only thing I could think of that didn't require energy or other people was to go to the mall. It had been so long since I'd done anything that felt normal. So I left. I spent the afternoon at the mall. I spent the evening eating at a favorite restaurant alone. I returned home to an empty house. It actually felt good to be alone.

People who mourn do so in different ways. At that moment, what I needed most was just to do something normal. I'm not sure anyone understood, but that was how I was processing my grief in that moment. As I read Jesus words, "*blessed are those who mourn, for they will be comforted*," I am reminded of that very real experience and how the comfort of God so overwhelmed me that day.

Grief is an essential component in blending families. Every single family member has experienced grief as a prelude to coming together as a family. As we look at the second beatitude, we will see the power of comfort in healing the blending family, both as individual members and as a whole. Begin now praying for each person in your family. While the grief may be long in the past, there are still moments when grief reappears. Trust the God of all comfort, to bring comfort, not only to each individual, but trust Him to comfort your family as well.

Day One

Blessed are the Mourners

"Blessed are those who mourn, for they will be comforted." Matthew 5:4

Jesus knew the pain and loss intrinsic in the earthly existence. Once again, Jesus mirrors the words of Isaiah. As Isaiah prophecies that the brokenhearted will be bound up and the captives and prisoners will be freed, there will also be a time when those who mourn will be comforted.

The contrast of this beatitude to the previous one is that the comfort is given as a future event. The implication is that there will be loss and mourning in this life. Jesus even said it again in John 16:33 as He prepared His disciples for His own death on the cross. *"In this world you will have trouble. But take heart! I have overcome the world."*

Trouble and loss in this world is inevitable. Once sin entered through Adam and Eve, so death, pain and loss followed. We are all on a journey that has brought us pain. You have lost a mate through death or divorce. Perhaps your relationships with your children are fractured. You no longer get to spend every holiday in a Norman Rockwell painting. There are empty chairs at your table. There are hurting children in your home. So Jesus spoke the truth when He declared that *"in **this world** you **will have** trouble."* Let's pause for a moment and take apart that passage.

Read John 16:17-33.

Circle the word "joy" or "rejoices" every time it appears in this passage.

Record everything you learn about the word "joy."

Note the contrasts involving "joy" or "rejoice."

What do you believe God is teaching you through this?

21

🕮 Read John 16:33.

Why does Jesus say He has "told you these things?"

What two things does Jesus tell His disciples about the world?

In this passage, Jesus is comforting His disciples in advance of the grief He knows they are soon to endure. They have lived alongside Jesus for the past three years. They have watched Him heal and deliver people from demons. They have heard Him speak profound truths about God. They have watched Him withdraw to His Father to pray. They have experienced miracles first-hand. Yet now, Jesus is speaking about something that sounds strange to them. His words are probably unnerving to them. They can feel their fear rising. They hear what Jesus is saying to them, yet they don't understand. He explains their coming grief. They still don't really understand. But each time Jesus discusses the grief they will bear, He follows it with a promise of joy.

One of the passages of scripture that is often used during funerals is *Psalm 23*. Let's look at *Psalm 23:4*. *"Even though I walk through the valley of the shadow of death, I will fear no evil, for you are with me; your rod and your staff they comfort me."* This is likely a very familiar Psalm to many of us. But have you really read it lately? Look at what David is saying. He says we will experience loss. But look at how we experience it.

First of all, David tells us that we *walk through* the valley. He doesn't say we stand in the valley. He doesn't say that we pitch a tent and remain in the valley. What he says is that we *walk through*. Do you see movement? The valley of the shadow of death is not a destination. It is a journey. We move into it, but we also move out of it. It will not last forever.

Psalm 30:5 is another indication. Again, David reminds us that weeping may remain for a night, but rejoicing comes in the morning. I learned that the very darkest part of the night occurs just before the sun begins to peek over the horizon. What a blessed hope for those who mourn. Remember, that when you feel like you are in the darkest moments, just watch the horizon. Look intently and expectantly. The sun is soon to appear.

Secondly, David says that what we walk through doesn't carry the full weight of death. Listen carefully. David doesn't say that we walk through the valley of death. He says we walk through the valley of the *shadow* of death. In God's grace, we only experience the shadow of death.

Go back for a moment with me to your childhood. Do you remember chasing your shadow? Was it you in that shadow? The answer is yes and no. While it was a depiction of you as a result of the position of the light source, it wasn't really you, literally. While you could see the outline of yourself, your features were undistinguishable. It was merely a shadow.

That is how David defines our experience of death on earth. He says that we walk through the valley, but in the valley is merely the shadow of death. Today you may be in the middle of the pain of your loss. It may not even be a physical death that you are enduring. It may be the pain of the death of a marriage. It may be the death of dream as your child has strayed so far away and is in a place you could never have imagined. Maybe it is the death of a relationship you once had with your children, but is now strained because of a divorce or a remarriage. I don't know the source of the "death" that you are experiencing today, but I have good news. Let's look at the second half of David's words.

Even though we will walk through the valley of the shadow of death, we have no need to fear evil. And evil does lurk in the face of death. Remember, death was the result of sin and sin the result of the evil one. So Satan loves death. And he loves to cripple us through death. But David said we don't have to be afraid of how the enemy wants to use death to cripple us. Why is that? Because God is with us.

God is with us. Present tense. David doesn't say God will be with us, even though we know God is already in the future. But we don't have to wait for God's presence. His presence is already with us. He comes with His rod and staff. Since this Psalm uses the analogy of a shepherd caring for the sheep, the fact that God comes with a rod and staff is significant. To a shepherd, the rod and staff serve specific purposes. The rod is used to protect the sheep against predators. It is a weapon to defend the sheep from the wolves who want to devour them. The staff is used to direct the sheep. The shepherd's hook is another name for the staff. It is often used to pull the sheep back onto the path of safety. So, David uses this illustration to help us understand how God keeps us safe from evil.

Finally, David tells us of God's comfort. It is His presence, His protection and His guidance that will comfort. I don't know about you, but I generally feel completely helpless when I go to comfort someone who is grieving. But in this passage I find hope. God doesn't come to our grief feeling helpless. He is actively involved in bringing comfort. As we return to Jesus' words in John, we find the same encouragement.

🐾 Look at John 16:33 again.

Why did Jesus tell the disciples "these things"?

One of the greatest things we have from the hand of God is peace. While we will study God's peace in-depth later in this study, for now, suffice it to say that real, lasting peace is centered on God's power at work in us through the Holy Spirit.

Enough for today. I hope you have found encouragement in the face of your own sense of loss, or the journey of someone in your family. We will pick up tomorrow to learn what Jesus has to say about being an overcomer.

Spend some time in your journal recording some of your thoughts and feelings. Perhaps your mourning is far in the past, but today's study has resurfaced some thoughts. Write out a prayer to God. Give Him anything that you have held onto. Thank Him for where He has brought you today. Release any current feelings of grief you are experiencing to Him. Consider:

How can I help my children and stepchildren with their grief?

How can I help my spouse when he or she grieves?

Often times, grief in a blending family is due to unfinished business. How can I handle this grief today? Meditate on *1 Peter 5:6-7*.

"Humble yourselves, therefore, under God's might hand that he may lift you up in due time. Cast all your anxiety on him because he cares for you." 1 Peter 5:6-7.

Day Two

You are an Overcomer

"I have told you these things, so that in me you may have peace. In this world you will have trouble. But take heart! I have overcome the world." John 16:33

Yesterday we looked at the words of Jesus telling us that in this world we will have trouble. While those words tend to bring us anxiety, what He says both before and after, should give us hope. Jesus doesn't leave us in the midst of our trouble. He says in John that we can take heart, because He has **overcome** the world. This beatitude tells us the same thing. **When** we mourn, we aren't left in our mourning. There will be comfort in the midst of the pain.

One of the passages of scripture that God gave my first husband and I in the midst of his illness and impending death was *2 Corinthians 1:3-11*. I continue to embrace the truth of that passage. It somehow helps me when trouble comes. It reminds me that I have a perfect Comforter in Christ. He doesn't comfort from afar as One who has never known affliction. Instead, He comforts as One who has walked the path of suffering. When He takes my hand, looks into my eyes and tells me He understands, I know He does because He has experienced the pain of loss and death and hurt and rejection.

But Paul doesn't stop with the comfort we receive from Christ in the passage in Corinthians. He goes on to encourage us in our own suffering. He reminds us our suffering will serve a purpose as well. We suffer **so that** we can then comfort others.

When you were going through your divorce, who brought you comfort? Was it old friends who were still married? Or did you find greater comfort in the words of those who had walked where you were now walking? There is great comfort in shared experiences. God allows you to walk through difficult days **so that** you can learn to more fully rely on Him for comfort. He also allows the journey **so that** you are a vessel for Him to use in the lives of others who are experiencing a similar journey.

There is comfort in Christ for those who mourn. As we look at the subject of mourning, it is important we understand that mourning is a process. It is not an event. We will look at each of the most widely accepted stages of grief in order for you to understand your own process or perhaps be able to help someone in your family who may be struggling.

We will begin today to look at the stages of grief. As we walk through each stage, be aware of your own feelings of loss, or perhaps the feeling of loss for someone in your household. I trust this will help you maneuver the waters of grief as you better understand that those who mourn, will be comforted.

Stages of Grief

Grief is not something that is quickly healed. Depending on the depth and source of the grief, you will likely continue to experience some level of grief for a period of time. Psychologists have defined seven stages of grief that everyone will likely cycle through. Those stages include unbelief, denial, anger, depression, guilt, bargaining, and acceptance. While there are variations and different words used to describe the stages among some psychologists, these are the most widely accepted. Grief is not an exact science. It is an emotional and physiological process we go through in order to find healing and wholeness after a loss. The stages do not necessarily occur in a certain order, may vary in duration from stage-to-stage and may vary in intensity. It is sometimes helpful to be able to identify the stage of grief in which you find yourself.

Sometimes we can get "stuck" in a stage. Being aware that you are "stuck" is important in learning how to move forward. Other people may try to define what your grieving process looks like. You need to trust yourself in the grief. However, there are times when you need a trusted friend or family member to help you see your grief in the light of healing. Remember, the purpose of grief is to help you heal. If you find yourself "stuck" in a stage or having a hard time moving forward, you might want to talk to a trusted friend, a pastor or a professional counselor to help you process your grief.

I liken the grief process to living in a wheel. While the loss is fresh, the wheel is very large and turns very slowly. Grief consumes you and it feels as though you will never move beyond where you are in this moment. As time passes and you learn to experience comfort in the grief, the wheel becomes smaller and begins to move more quickly. You may move between stages more quickly and the intensity of the stage is not as dramatic.

When considering the dynamics of your blending family, you may want to consider the stages of grief. There may be members of your family who still move in and out of stages. Also, consider that your family as a whole may be in a grieving process. That may sound strange, but think about it. Your family unit was formed as a result of a loss. As your family begins, and even years later, as it grows and develops, there may be moments when you are reminded that you are not nuclear. Perhaps, even as a family you may be grieving the loss of what some people may term, a "normal" family.

Being able to recognize what you may be experiencing is a stage in the grief process, can help you in your healing process. It is normal to experience the feelings associated with the stages of grief. We will briefly look at the stages and how they may manifest.

Disbelief

This stage usually occurs early in the grief process. Disbelief involves the rational mind trying to process what seems completely unreal. The medical diagnosis cannot be right. There must be something less serious that is causing the symptoms. The accident victim has somehow been misidentified and isn't your relative after all. Your boss really didn't mean that you are losing your job. Tomorrow morning he will realize what he's done and come crawling back to you. There could not have been a fire that has claimed your home. There must be a mistake.

Disbelief is how we respond when the thing we think could never happen to us, does happen to us. We really can't make sense out of it. This will probably be the predecessor of the inevitable "why?" question.

Sometimes disbelief is also described as shock or numbness. Your thoughts don't make sense. You are processing what you hear, but it just doesn't seem like a reality. Sometimes onlookers are critical when this occurs. People who are in this stage of grief may appear un-phased by the tragedy or loss. But in reality, they have not been able to fully grasp the reality of the loss. They are numb. Some people describe this stage as "simply going through the motions."

Psychologists would tell us that this stage allows us to do what we have to do in the face of loss. Planning a funeral service for a loved one who has died suddenly is impossible in light of the event of loss, yet we are able to function and accomplish the task.

🐾 Have you experienced disbelief as a blending family? What are some examples? Be particularly aware of your children's perspective.

As parents and step-parents, how can you help your children through this stage?

Denial

There is a fine line between disbelief and the next stage which is denial. Often times if the loss is unexpected, the stage of denial can be longer. If the divorce or death that left a single-parent family was unexpected, the denial may be longer. Your mind knows the person is gone, but you live expecting the person to return. In death, your mind knows the person is gone, but you sometimes find yourself expecting them to come through the door. In divorce, there is sometimes one spouse who hangs onto the hope that the divorce will not be final or there may be a chance of reconciliation. Many times in divorce, the children who are experiencing grief can remain in the denial stage for a long time. They may not fully give up hope that their parents will reconcile. It may be that the children don't move out of this stage until one or both of the parents actually remarry.

We will stop here for today. These first two stages of grief are likely a vague memory for you. Your blending family has become the focus of your life. But remember that stages can be briefly revisited. Sometimes circumstances or events can trigger a return to a stage of grief. Being aware of the stages might prove helpful if you or someone in your family is struggling.

🙐 Have you dealt with this stage with your blending family? If so, what are some observations you have?

How can you help your family as a whole process this stage of grief?

Are there children in your family who are particularly prone to express this stage? How do they act it out?

What are some practical ideas you may have for helping your family through this stage?

Spend time thanking God for the comfort He brought you and your family in your loss. Thank Him for His presence and power in your new family. Ask Him to help you embrace the new members of your blending family with love and compassion.

If you are struggling with someone in your family, it might help if you thought about them through the lens of their loss. Try to understand their pain and what they endured before becoming a part of your family. Pray for them, that God will continue to use you to bring comfort and healing.

More tomorrow.

Day Three

And the Grief Goes On

As we begin today, I would ask that you spend some time in prayer before starting the study. Remember our beatitude for the week: *"Blessed are those who mourn for they will be comforted."* Today we will resume our study of the stages of grief. As we begin with today's stage, come with a willing heart to hear and understand God's message to you.

Anger

This stage is an expression of anger at the loss. The recipient of the anger, however, can vary. Anger can even be turned inward. It may feel inappropriate to express anger, or the person may not know where to express their anger, so they turn it inward. Sometimes self-destructive behavior is a symptom of internalized anger. Anger can also be aimed at another. Even in death, there can be anger at the one who died. Sometimes anger might explode out of situations where the missing spouse would have handled a circumstance.

Early in the grief process children may express anger. They may revisit this anger later on toward a step-parent. This may come as a surprise because during courtship, the child seemed to like the adult their parent was dating. Understanding that the step-parent now becomes an obstacle to the reconciliation of the parents may initiate the anger stage of grief for the child. They can no longer remain in denial. There is now a new person who has joined the family and dashed the hopes of reconciliation in the eyes of the child.

An important point to remember is that the anger directed toward the new step-parent may not be personal, but situational. They are not angry at the person as much as they are angry over the position that person has filled in the new family structure. Understanding this can often help the new step-parent feel less defensive and better able to help build a positive relationship with the child. While the anger will likely be temporary, remember that the child may move in and out of the anger stage. One important point to remember about grief is that once a stage has been experienced that doesn't mean it will never be revisited. Even years later, angry outbursts may be attributed to grief.

There is another important point to remember as children express grief. Often times the most honest feelings are expressed toward the parent who feels "safe." Sometimes in divorce, the children perceive one parent as the one who left. For them, the parent who left may cause the children to feel like that parent might not actually return at all. There has not yet been a pattern of visitation established, and the children may feel very uncertain and insecure about the non-custodial parent's role in their lives now that they no longer live in the household. The parent who remains is often viewed by the children as the parent who has stayed and will not likely leave. The feelings of anger that must be expressed may very well be expressed toward the parent who remains. Understanding this will help the remaining parent who may feel overwhelmed because of being left as well as having to deal with the outbursts of angry children.

Anger can sometimes be the most difficult stage to deal with. Anger in itself is a necessary expression of life. Paul, in his letter to the Ephesians, says it like this: *"**In your anger** do not sin. Do not let the sun go down while you are still angry, and do not give the devil a foothold." (Ephesians 4:26-27).* Anger is an inevitable part of life. Even Jesus expressed anger when He overturned the tables of the moneychangers in the Temple. But Paul exhorts us to manage our anger in such a way that we don't sin. Anger can be expressed in very hurtful, damaging ways, both verbally and physically.

There is great wisdom in "the countdown" some people exercise in their anger. Words are like toothpaste. Once out of the tube, it can never be put back in. Same with words. Once expressed, the damage they do cannot be undone. As the proverbial saying goes, "you can't un-ring the bell."

Anger can also be expressed in a way that is physically harmful. A bloody nose at the other end of an angry fist may come to mind. But also anger unexpressed and turned inward can manifest itself in self-destructive or careless behavior. I once had a friend who said, "You don't want an angry 16-year-old behind the wheel of a car." Anger can alter our ability to make rational decisions and choices and can also numb our ability to make careful decisions.

Is anger an issue in your household? If so, pause here and take some time to dissect it. Here are a few questions that might help you process the anger you see or feel in your home.

&. If there is anger in the home, can you identify the source?

Is there a person that is particularly susceptible to outbursts of anger?

Is there a specific trigger for the anger?

Is there a member of the household that seems to be the recipient of the angry outbursts?

Helping your family understand that there are certain occasions when anger might be a temptation can help. Perhaps tensions are higher when the ex-spouse is coming to pick up children for visitation. Simply knowing that this is a recipe for a potential angry outburst might help prevent it.

The beauty of God's Word is that it not only provides instruction and encouragement in how to live life well, but also gives suggestions for handling the flesh. While anger isn't a sin, it is certainly a short hallway to provide an opportunity for the enemy to take control. If you know that a certain situation is going to bring the opportunity for anger, perhaps coming together as a couple in prayer and asking God to take the anger away and replace it with His peace will give you just what you need for a pleasant exchange of the children. After all, the children are already feeling anxious about the interchange you and your ex-spouse may have. They can feel the anger rising. Think of the comfort you can provide your children in the transition if they leave under the umbrella of a peaceful exchange.

So what can you do in this situation to prevent the anger from exploding? It may seem impossible with today's crazy schedules, but simply allowing some quiet down-time for children before the exchange can help. If your family is running in the back door while the doorbell is ringing announcing the arrival of your ex-spouse likely adds to the tension. Providing a calm environment can help calm the children's anxiety. Making sure you and your children are home in plenty of time to be ready for the exchange can help prevent angry outbursts. Make this a priority as you would any other appointment. Also, keeping a consistent routine for the exchange helps. Maybe there is a special suitcase dedicated solely for those weekend visits.

Communication between parents is often the cause of angry exchanges. Perhaps the two parents could communicate about logistics or anything else that might cause tension before the exchange. If those issues could be handled separately, the child is able to experience an anger-free transition. Always remember to keep the welfare and comfort of the child at the forefront. You may have a curt word to the ex-spouse who is always late for pick-up. Refrain. Save those conversations until it is just the two of you out of ear-shot of the children. You may have some instructions for homework that needs to be finished. Discuss those expectations before the exchange.

This all probably sounds overwhelming. And it will be an inconvenience for you and your ex-spouse. But remember, the goal is to provide an anger-free transition for your child. Let them see their parents parting as amicably as possible. The reality is that your ex-spouse may not be willing to cooperate. You have no control over what they do or how they react. It would be reasonable for you to talk to them earlier in the week and explain that you are working on ways to make the transition more pleasant for the children. However, they may be unwilling. You cannot control what they choose. But, for the well-being of your children, as much as possible, do all you can to make the transition as pleasant for your children as you can.

When anger rises, especially with children, they need a constructive way to vent. This is true of any children, whether in a blending family or not. There are appropriate ways to express anger and inappropriate ways to express it. But certainly there is angry energy that needs to be released.

One activity we found to be particularly helpful involved nails, hammer, a board and safety goggles. We kept a long 2 x 4 in the garage and bag of 10 penny nails, along with a hammer and goggles available for anyone who might need it. We might find any one of the children in the backyard, having drug out the board and nails just hammering away. I could always tell the level of anger based on the force exerted on the board. Sometimes, the anger wouldn't even hit the nails. Just beating on the board was enough. We found that to be an appropriate physical expression of anger. Sometimes we might suggest that one (or more) of the children get on their bike and ride as fast as they could. Make sure they have a safe place to ride. When they are "in the anger" they are not as aware as they should be of their surroundings.

Additionally, helping the children be able to identify their feeling and perhaps even verbalize why they have the feeling can help give them power over their anger. Parents can help by modeling healthy expressions of anger. Children need to know that adults get angry as well. They also need to see the adults they trust expressing their anger in appropriate ways.

We will deal with the remaining stages of grief tomorrow. Anger is usually a big one. And not all anger is grief related. But perhaps some of the discussion about anger will help you and your family better understand and process any anger that exists in your home.

The most powerful way to diffuse anger is to talk about why you are angry. Sometimes this requires a brief time of cooling down. But giving all family members the freedom to express why they are angry will help give them power over a feeling they might think can't be controlled. Open, honest, conversation, done in gentleness will bring your family to a deeper place of understanding and unity. Allow everyone the freedom to share why they are angry. Help them understand their feeling, and give them opportunity to express their anger. Sometimes, as the adult, we need to step back and be removed from the conversation. Try not to take other's anger personally. There may be many things behind their expression of anger. Try to be objective, and hear their heart.

As a couple, find a time to go to each of your children's rooms and pray over the rooms, their beds, the areas where they play or interact. Pray for God's peace to flood each room. Allow the Holy Spirit to guide you as pray. Be sensitive to any specifics He may be directing for you to pray for each child in your home.

🔖 Think of a time you felt angry and retrospectively feel you didn't handle it well. Describe that event.

If you could have a do-over, what would you have done differently?

As we close today, let anger in your home be a matter of prayer. Ask God to pour out His grace and peace in your home. Allow Him to so overwhelm you and your family with His love that you can begin to release the grip that anger has on you and your family.

Day Four

Will the Grief Ever End?

The topic we covered yesterday might have left you feeling a bit heavy and burdened. Anger is always a difficult subject to discuss. I hope you were able to spend some time in prayer to work on any anger that exists chronically in your family. We will begin today with heavy topics as well. As we step into this day's study of mourning, allow God to open your heart to hear the word He has for you today.

Guilt

Guilt is the stage where grief asks if you were somehow to blame for what happened. Perhaps there is guilt because it might somehow be my fault that the loss occurred. If I had insisted that my spouse visit the doctor sooner, the disease could have been diagnosed and treated earlier with a different outcome. If I had been a more attentive spouse, then perhaps my mate would not have chosen to leave the marriage. As in most stages, pain accompanies the guilt.

Although spiritual guilt can be a stumbling block, guilt in a loss can be a beginning to healing. Perhaps you could have done something differently. In the case of a spouse lost through divorce, this is the stage where you begin to release any perceived victimization and begin to take ownership of your contribution to the break-up of your marriage. In death, this stage may lead you to a point of realization that you did, in fact, do all you knew to do in order to help your spouse survive. Perhaps you lost a mate in an automobile accident that occurred because they were running an errand for you. Guilt will certainly take you to the point of "if only." This is good place to pause and consider what God's Word has to say about processing past events.

Paul spends a fair bit of ink telling the recipients of his letters to beware of worry. While worry may not seem like a relative of guilt, I think they make nice cousins. Worry is a divided state of mind. It is allowing yourself to live in bondage to what could happen in the future at the expense of the experiences of today's journey. While worry is bondage to the future, guilt is bondage to the past. Worrying about tomorrow does absolutely nothing to prevent the occurrence of the objects of your worry. In the same way, guilt over the past does nothing to change what is behind you. Both of these views do nothing but rob you of the joy and peace God desires that you experience today. Let's spend a few minutes with Paul, and see what he has to say about the past.

📖 Read Philippians 3:13-14.

What are the two contrasts Paul makes?

What does he say about these two "times"?

What is Paul "pressing on" toward?

Paul reminds the Philippians that God has something ahead for them. God has a plan and purpose for you and your new family as well. What the enemy would love to do, is to keep you buried in guilt so you can't see the future God has for you.

Let this stage of guilt be a springboard to take you out of the "if only's" and spur you on toward what God has for you and your new family. Take ownership of the things that you would have liked to have done differently. Release those things to God. Allow Him to forgive you and help you see His hand of redemption. This is the beginning of overcoming the hurdle of guilt. Recognize that this can be a true turning point in your healing process.

Depression

This stage of grief must be handled carefully. It is important to make a very real distinction when using the word depression. Depression resulting from a loss is often referred to as situational depression. On the other hand, clinical depression is independent of circumstances and is largely physiological in nature. If you are suffering from clinical depression that does not go away, please seek professional help from a trusted psychiatrist or psychologist.

However, if your depression is a result of loss, it is transient and is a normal stage in the grief process. Depression as a stage of grief generally occurs once the reality of the loss has fully set in. In the case of death, the realization that the person is truly gone and will not return brings deep sadness and longing. The depression may be the result of the realization that the family you had so cherished, will never be the same. Children will live in separate households. The dreams you had for your family will not look like you had always imagined. You may be grieving the loss of security. You may feel as though you are now "marked" and will always be viewed as broken. You may be grieving the loss of what you have always known as "normal."

In the grief process, depression may actually be a positive turn for you. Realizing the truth of your loss may be the beginning of acceptance. Once you have fully given in to the reality of the loss, you can begin to recover. How you process your depression is also important.

Simply giving in to the sadness that makes you want to stay in bed may be briefly necessary, but over the long term will prevent you from moving forward in your healing. Processing your feelings is important in depression. Many people find healing through keeping a journal. Even children can keep a journal. Journals don't have to be written documents. Younger children, or children who wish to express themselves without many words might find comfort in drawing or painting their feelings.

If you are helping your children through this stage, you can aid their progress by helping them identify feelings they might not be able to verbally identify. As they are willing to share their journals or pictures, you can ask questions that will help you understand what they are feeling. Children sometimes do not have a full vocabulary for their feelings. You can help them process by helping them understand what they are feeling based on what you observe in their drawing or writing. See this stage as an opportunity for you to grow as a family by processing your feelings openly and honestly.

One activity we found helpful in the early days of our blending family was butcher paper on the dining table. We kept crayons next to our large dining table (crayons only because markers bleed through the paper). We completely covered the table with butcher paper. We would write a word or phrase in the middle of the paper. The kids then had the freedom to draw or write anything they wanted to about the word or phrase. Once we explained the concept to the kids, we really didn't have to say much about the paper. They would notice when it was there and respond. We might leave the paper on the table for a week or two allowing the kids to draw or write whenever they wanted to.

You can choose whatever you want for the phrase. It could be an opportunity to process something, or it could be simply a place to express. For example, you might use the phrase "how I feel about being a family." Be ready to discuss any struggles you see emerging as the children add to the paper. You might decide to use the phrase "places I'd like to go on vacation this year." Always find a time for the family to come together and talk about what has been drawn. By the way, mom and dad should participate as well.

One year we even took this idea one step further. I purchased a white cotton tablecloth and put it on the dining table for a couple of weeks before Christmas. I used fabric crayons and let everyone draw or write about Christmas memories they had. It was a lot of fun, and the kids enjoy looking at the tablecloth even years later.

You might also make up your own game of Pictionary. Give children an opportunity to express their feelings. Just be careful with competition. In this setting, it does not need to be about winning and losing. There is simply freedom for children to express their feelings, and pictures can sometimes be a good indicator of the source of the feeling.

But the goal is to provide an opportunity for everyone to process their feelings. Understanding and identifying the feelings provide opportunity to process them. It is easy to get stuck in depression. Providing a safe place for family members to process their feelings will help keep the healing process moving forward.

👣 Have you ever felt situational depression? Describe what happened.

How did you overcome it?

Is someone in your blending family struggling with depression? Describe what you see in them.

Spend some time brainstorming. What do you think might help them?

Together with your spouse, design an action plan to begin helping anyone in your family who is struggling with situational depression. Be flexible. Do not be afraid to abandon an idea that is not working and try something else. Be sensitive and allow God to work.

Once again, as we close today's time together, go to the Lord and let Him have any feelings that are holding you back from your healing. Unresolved feelings can definitely get in the way of progress within your new family. Let God use your feelings to bring you the comfort you long for. As we close, meditate on *Matthew 5:4* out of the Message.

> *"You're blessed when you feel you've lost what is most dear to you. Only then can you be embraced by the One most dear to you."*

Allow the most dear One to embrace you today.

Day Five

Let the Healing Begin

There are two final stages of grief we will discuss today. Then I will provide some suggestions for how to overcome and experience the comfort God has for you. Continue to pray for your family members by name and ask God to help you better understand each individual and their unique journey. Let God use you as the vessel for healing for those in your family who are still hurting.

Bargaining

There is a phrase in the military that refers to "foxhole confessions." The idea is that when a soldier is in a foxhole with bullets flying overhead and bombs exploding all around, he is faced quite boldly with his own mortality. I often wonder how many soldiers surrender to the ministry while in a foxhole. When death seems imminent, we can begin to make deals with God. Africa would likely be overrun with missionaries if everyone who bargained with God in a moment of desperation actually followed through on the deal.

Lest we think such bargaining is only a current phenomenon, let me take you to a story in the Bible where a great King bargained with God. King Hezekiah was a King of Judah. He was one of the few Kings who followed God and was considered a good king. The story of King Hezekiah tells us that he did what was right in the eyes of the Lord (*2 Kings 18:3*) and he trusted in the Lord, the God of Israel (*2 Kings 18:5*). In time however, we find that the good King had fallen ill. Here is where we pick up the story.

Read 2 Kings 20:1-6.

Can you relate with Hezekiah? Reflect on a time you have bargained with God when life seemed hopeless.

Hezekiah did not want to die. He bargained with God to let him live. When we have lost someone, we may feel the same desire to bargain with God. Bargaining can happen in the midst of losing someone. If you are experiencing the illness of a loved one, you may bargain with God to extend their life. If you are going through a divorce, perhaps you are bargaining with God or even with that person to extend the relationship.

Bargaining is an attempt to change the outcome. You and your children may have tried to bargain with one another or with God during this stage of grief. However, as a newly

38

blending family, you are likely beyond this stage. Even so, there may be moments when you vacillate between "if only" and "what if." When things in your new family become difficult, it is easy to slip back into the feelings of bargaining.

In grief, the outcome of the situation has already been secured. Death has ended a relationship. Divorce has taken you and your previous mate into new relationships and you are both forming new families. You may see bargaining in your blending family as an attempt to control. Everything may feel out-of-control, and bargaining with others in your family, or even with yourself, may feel like regaining some control.

With children, bargaining in a blending family may sound like "I wish." Children wish you and their other parent had not split up. They wish you had not remarried. They wish they didn't have to go from house to house to see their parents. They wish they did not have stepsiblings. They wish things were not so tense between you and their other parent.

It is important to allow children to process these feelings out loud. Once again, you can help them by providing a safe place for them to openly and honestly express their feelings. There is really no way to help them be "rational" at this point. It is more important to just listen to them, affirm their feelings and let go of the need to explain or fix the situation. The result is fixed, and their feelings are real.

Acceptance

This is the goal of the grief process. Once the feelings have come full circle, there is a time when you accept the loss. You are then able to move forward with your life without the person who is absent. Understand that acceptance is **not** denial that the person existed or was part of your life. It is, however, the freedom to move on with your life without that person being a part of it. Helping children especially to know that acceptance does not require that they forget the person or deny the relationship even though things are different now. It is more a matter of reframing how the relationship is expressed.

For example, children of divorce now must accept two households. They no longer live with both biological parents in the same home. Each parent is establishing a new home and a new family system. Whether parents remain single or remarry, the children are relating to each parent differently.

Knowing the stages of grief, and understanding that these feelings and experiences are normal may help you and your new family move forward. The stages may reappear at times. Don't be surprised if, during a season change in the life of one of your family members that a return to one or more of the stages will occur. A child who has lost a parent may experience one or more of the stages even after years have passed. Sometime children re-process their loss when they graduate from high school or when they get married. Realizing that grief is a process and not a goal, will help everyone in the family in their ability to empathize.

So wherever you are in the grief process, you can be confident that you do not grieve as one who has no hope. You have a Comforter who is ever-present providing hope and healing. So how can you manage your own emotions as you grieve? Here are a few practical suggestions.

Talk to God. Be open and honest with Him. Discuss your feelings with Him as if He were a cherished friend. He can hear your anger or pain. He understands your grief. And He can help you through it. He knew before you did about what would happen to you.

God has gone before you and He goes behind you. *"You hem me in – behind and before; you have laid your hand upon me" Psalm 139:5.* Nothing surprises God. He knew before the foundation of the world that you would be exactly where you are at this moment. But better still, He has made a provision for you, where you are at this moment. He has everything you need. He has prepared the path ahead of you, and He's got your back. You don't have to endure this alone. He is with you every step.

Keep a journal. Sometimes it's difficult to follow your own progress. It's a bit like gaining weight. While I see myself every day, I may not notice as the pounds pile on. But when I see someone I haven't seen in a while, their words may not tell me I've put on weight, but their face sure does. In the midst of your grief, you may not see progress. But progress is happening. By keeping a journal, you have a snapshot of where you have been. You may be pleasantly surprised at how far you've come. Writing down your thoughts and feelings is a good way to map your progress. It will also help keep you on track. Conversely, it will likely be a good indicator if you are stuck or digressing.

Do one thing every day that makes you happy. In the midst of your grief, you may believe that there will never again be anything that will bring you joy. Try to spend some of your energy every day doing something that you enjoy. It may be something as simple as enjoying a cup of coffee on your back patio in the morning. But find something each day that will remind you that life is continuing, and you can find joy in the midst of your pain. Realize that this kind of self-care is important and is not a selfish behavior. It may be just what you need to get through another day.

Remind yourself that nothing lasts forever. The pain you are experiencing today will eventually fade. In the early days of grief you may believe you will never, ever feel good again. But you will. I remember vividly the day I heard the birds singing again. I knew they had been there all along, singing their little beaks off. But I had not heard them in the tomb of my grief. Then, there was that day, when I walked outside and there they were. Singing. And I actually heard them. In that moment I shed tears of gratitude instead of pain.

Let yourself feel. People have a way of trying to help you through your grief from the outside. The trouble is, they are on the outside. They really don't know what's best for you. Only you know what's best for you. People will likely give you lots of advice. They have good intentions because they don't want to see you hurt. They love you and want to help you. But sometimes they share advice that is not helpful. They want you to hurry through your grief. They tell you that it is time for you to get out. They suggest a variety of activities. You will feel better if you'll get involved in, well, you fill in the blank. They want to stop your tears. They don't want you to talk about your loss. They don't understand how you can laugh sometimes when you remember your loss. But it is your grief. Let the feelings come and then let them go. Trust yourself to move through your feelings at the pace that feels best for you.

Help others. It is easy to become so deeply entrenched in your own grief, that you lose sight of others. When the Pharisees asked Jesus about the greatest commandment, He replied that loving God is the first and greatest commandment. But He quickly added that the second greatest commandment is that we love others as we love ourselves. If you really want to begin to experience healing and hope, reach out and help someone else. It doesn't have to be big or difficult. But simply helping someone else will bring a new perspective, and move the focus off of you for a while.

Give yourself the freedom to say no. It takes a tremendous amount of energy to grieve. After I lost my husband, a friend sent me an article on grief that gave a statistic that surprised me. In the article, the author said that it takes 86% of our energy just to grieve. I don't know exactly where and how that statistic originated. It may not even be accurate, but I know it helped me understand why I had such a hard time getting even the simplest task completed. If the stat is true, that means you only have 14% of your energy left to do everything else your life demands. For me, it included working, taking care of my boys who were hurting, keeping the house and the yard done, grocery shopping and cooking, laundry, bill paying, car servicing and home maintenance. I never realized how much easier life was with two adults working together.

Realizing that you don't have 100% of your energy to focus on the tasks of daily life gives you permission to choose carefully what you do with the energy you do have. I have a friend who reminds me often that there is a period at the end of the word "no." Not a comma, but a period. That means, when you need to say no to something or someone, it can just be no. Period. No explanation is necessary. It's just no.

As we end this week's study, I hope you feel equipped and empowered to work through any unfinished grief in you or your family. All of life is a process and we never actually arrive. I do believe that God is so much more interested in our daily journey than He is in any kind of an overall outcome. Once we become His, He begins the process of preparing us for eternity.

I know this week has not had us in the Word very much, but understanding mourning and grief is important in helping us understand what God's comfort means for us. Close out this week in prayer with your spouse. Spend time praying together for all of your family. Every single one of you has experienced grief in one way or another. Ask God to give you insight into anyone in your family who needs a special touch this week. Blessings on you as you persevere.

Week Three

Blessed are the Meek

"Blessed are the meek, for they will inherit the earth." Matthew 5:5

We had just sat down around the table for our annual family Thanksgiving celebration. We were hosting family for the evening feast. We were enjoying time together, laughing and, of course, eating. The doorbell rang. I quickly did a check around the table wondering who we had forgotten about. But everyone was present. What an odd time for someone to be at the door. Dinner on Thanksgiving evening. So I went to the door, which was in plain eye and ear shot of our guests at the dining room table. Standing before me was a courier with a court summons. Over the past few months, there had been some changes with our family, and my husband and his ex-wife were altering some of the arrangements for the girls. What we thought was being handled amicably without having to secure attorneys and go to court, had obviously taken a new turn. Of course his ex-wife knew what our Thanksgiving plans were because of making holiday arrangements for the girls to see both parents. This was just another reminder that we were not nuclear.

At *family [re]design*, we have spent time researching the needs of blending families. While some of the issues they face are the same as any other family, they also have issues that are unique to blending families. We have discovered that the number one issue blending families deal with, particularly in the early days of blending, revolve around the ex-spouse relationship.

So what does the Bible have to say about dealing with ex-spouses? You are probably scratching your head, trying to recall some obscure passage in the Old Testament about a dysfunctional family (there were **many**) involving an ex-spouse. Keep scratching your head, because although the Old Testament is **full** of men who had multiple wives and fractured families, pitting brother against brother, incest and other atrocities, there is really no clear example of dealing with an ex-spouse, per se.

While Moses, Jesus and Paul all three addressed the topic of divorce, the Bible doesn't really record any accounts of divorce and remarriage that I can find. But the Bible does give us a great amount of insight on how God expects us to deal with others. And He doesn't make exceptions for ex-spouses who are making life a nightmare. He simply gives a guide for how He wants us to live. I believe Jesus gives us a clear example of how to rightly relate with others, including an ex-spouse. As you study this week's topic, I encourage you to do so with a prayerful heart. Ask God to speak to you. Some of the things He says to you may be difficult to hear and even harder to put into practice. Ask God for the grace and power to be instructed and guided by His Spirit.

Day One

Meekness ... with an Ex-Spouse?

As we open this week's study, we need to start at the beginning. We must gain a clear understanding of what it means to be meek. While perhaps the word conjures images of weakness and unwillingness to stand up against others, nothing could be further from the true meaning. While indeed this word means gentle and self-controlled, not condescending or malicious, it certainly doesn't connote weakness. Those who are truly meek are influential against oppression, evil and violence not because they "fight back" but because they are able to take a stand in gentle power that builds up rather than tears down.

Jesus was the perfect example of meekness. While He was always gentle and self-controlled, He never once backed down against oppression or violence. He was a champion for those who were being abused or taken advantage of. He stood up for those who could not stand up for themselves. In fact, the very purpose of His assignment on earth was to provide for mankind, what we could not provide for ourselves. He secured our eternal salvation by His death on the cross. When you champion the cause of those who are oppressed or who need someone to stand up for them, you are expressing the kind of meekness that Jesus said will allow you to inherit the earth.

When confronted with the complexities of a blending family, meekness is essential. While you may have relationships with ex-spouses or stepchildren that push you to the brink of your patience, consider how Jesus dealt with those whom He found difficult.

He always stood on the truth. While we are human and could never live the consistent life that Jesus did, we can look to Him as our example and trust the Holy Spirit to empower us. The truth of God's Word tells us how we are to respond to difficult people. When dealing with the Pharisees, Jesus never backed down from the truth. When you are dealing with ex-spouses or stepchildren who are difficult, know that you can stand on the truth you find in the Word. What does God's Word demand? That we love others. We are to love those who hate us and pray for those who persecute us. While the Bible speaks of spiritual persecution, we know when dealing with exes, we, too may experience personal persecution. At least that's how it may feel. Perhaps in their anger they are persecuting our character. Perhaps out of their hurt, they may even rail against us to our children.

But Jesus showed us a unique combination of two things that could be considered opposites. He was the embodiment of grace, yet He never stepped back from the truth. When He encountered sin, He never apologized it away, or diminished its power to destroy, yet He shared the words of truth in a cocoon of love and grace. He never diminished the heart of the sinner, He only brought out the truth of their sin.

This week we will look at truths to help us deal with our ex-spouse. While some divorces result in amicable relationships, and others are out-and-out wars, we must recognize, that regardless, the relationship you once shared has changed. While you once were a team, bound together by love for each other, you now find yourselves at odds. Many things work against you as you strive to build a new relationship after your divorce. So how can you find the strength to live out the principle of meekness? We will turn to Paul's letter to the Corinthians for some insights.

📖 *Read 2 Corinthians 10:1-7.*

How does Paul begin this passage?

It appears as though Paul has something difficult he needs to share with the Corinthians. Before he even introduces his thoughts, he implores them on behalf of the meekness and gentleness of Christ.

What is the issue that Paul introduces in *2 Corinthians 10:2*?

What does Paul tell them in *2 Corinthians 10:3*?

What does he say about the weapons we use to wage war?

Apparently the Corinthian believers are struggling to understand that the way of the world is contrary to the way of God. While looking at life from an earthly perspective, they are oblivious to the real war they are encountering.

Paul says that we do not wage war as the world does. We don't fight with worldly weapons. This can be applied to dealing with an ex-spouse. The world says to be vindictive. Take what rightly belongs to you. Hurt them for what they've done to you. Or discard them if you are no longer interested in sharing a life with them. The world fights in courtrooms, demanding to win. The world fights with angry words and bitterness. The world uses children as weapons in the arsenal for piling more hurt and pain on the one who has hurt us.

But Paul implies, as Christ-followers, we should be different in how we wage war, and that we have tools at our disposal which are not of this world. Look again at what he says: *"On the contrary, they (the weapons we use) have the divine power to demolish strongholds.*

We demolish arguments and every pretension that sets itself up against the knowledge of God, and we take captive every thought to make it obedient to Christ." 2 Corinthians 10:4b-5.

🔊 Perhaps this is a good place to pause, and meditate on this passage. How can you use this passage to pray? What are the "thoughts" God may be prompting you to "make obedient to Christ"?

Paul contrasts the world with those of us who pledge our allegiance to Christ. Some might call this way of thinking and acting as a complete shift in thinking. What if you were able to filter your relationship with your ex-spouse through this passage? How would your relationship be different today?

Paul begins by telling us that we don't wage war with the same attitudes as the world does. What would be contrary to the world's ideas about how to handle a broken relationship resulting in a broken marriage? Instead of revenge, the Word teaches we are to love our enemy and pray for those who persecute us. Instead of getting our own way, we pursue what's best for another. Jesus' second greatest commandment tells us to love our neighbor as we love ourselves.

Let me pause here to make a slight clarification. Loving your enemy and praying for them does not mean you allow yourself to be mistreated. Love your neighbor *as you love yourself* is Christ's command. But oftentimes when the divorce battle heats us, we become so focused on what we want and getting revenge, or taking our mate to the cleaners, that we forget to focus on a work God wants to do in us and through us. Be very careful of your motives when deciding how you will pursue your divorce agreement. And there will likely be additional negotiations along the way as the children get older and visitation and financial matters may become more complex.

The weapons we use have divine power. I can hear what you are thinking. There is no way you can overcome your hurt, anger and frustration at your ex-spouse. You feel powerless to treat them kindly and fairly. But that's where the divine part steps in. God is not asking you to wage war in your own strength using your own weapons. He's not even asking you to use your will-power to refrain from responding as the world would. He is offering His weapons which have divine power. Trust Him. Allow Him to take over all your feelings, and begin to do a work in you. Allow Him to provide the weapons for warfare.

Demolish strongholds. It is important to understand a stronghold is considered something Satan has captured. What begins as an area of our life where we are not completely surrendered to the Lordship of Christ, becomes fertile ground for the enemy to step in. I like the analogy of a salesman at the door. Years ago, there was a profession of individuals who would go door-to-door selling everything from vacuum cleaners to encyclopedias. They were masters at getting in the door. You've heard the phrase "just get a foot in the door"? That must be where it began. If they could talk their way from the front porch into your living room, their chances of making a sale increased exponentially. They were so good at what they did, they made it almost impossible to say no.

While I am **not** claiming that door-to-door sales is demonic by any means, I do think it gives a great picture of how cunning Satan can be when it comes to gaining ground in our hearts. If he can whisper in our ear just enough to soften us to his temptation, it doesn't take him long to make himself at home in our heart, capturing valuable ground. These are the strongholds; the areas where Satan has slithered his way in with slippery words and deceiving thoughts and has taken you beyond where you ever thought you would be. These are the areas of your life and thoughts where you must rely on the power of Christ in you to overcome, yet the enemy has come in and taken over. He has occupied a stronghold in your mind.

But look at what Paul has to say. The weapons at our disposal are divine and are powerful enough to demolish the strongholds. Satan can have no more power over your thoughts and attitudes than you allow him to. Notice these weapons also demolish arguments and every pretension that sets itself up against the knowledge of God.

Consider what it is that generally defines your communication with your ex-spouse. Arguments. You argue about the children. You argue about the schedule. You argue about finances. But realize you are not a slave to the argumentative nature. These divine weapons demolish arguments. Paul doesn't say the weapons stop arguments. He says the weapons *demolish* the arguments. The arguments don't even exist anymore. While there still may be things over which you disagree, the arguing can be destroyed. After all, isn't an argument just a verbal battle where your strongest desire is to win? Perhaps when we begin to understand that the mind of Christ calls us to look at our ex-spouse through His eyes, we can step back and look at the reasons why we are embroiled in an argument. Is the financial disagreement you are having about what's best for taking care of the children, or is it more about you fighting for a financial advantage? Is the fight over the schedule based on finding something that will work best for everyone or is it more about you wanting control? Look at the root of the argument, and ask God to speak to your heart. Ask Him to use His divine weapons to do away with your desire to argue.

These weapons also demolish all pretense which sets itself up against the knowledge of God. What exactly does that mean? Being pretentious means one is showing or portraying an attitude of superiority. The pretensions Paul addresses sets itself up against the knowledge of God. So are you valuing your own attitudes as superior to God's design for relationships? Do you behave as though you are justified in how you treat your ex-spouse? Paul says these pretensions can be destroyed by the divine weapons of God.

And finally, as the battle for your thoughts and attitudes rages, Christ has the power to take your every thought captive. Your Godly walk begins with your thoughts. *As a man thinks, so he is*. When it comes to dealing with your ex-spouse, how often do you stop and purposefully give God your thoughts? When the encounter with them begins to escalate, are you able to breathe a prayer and ask God to wield His weapon to take every thought captive?

This is a good place to stop for today. As we close, I want you to find a way to have some time alone, undistracted. Begin your time by praying, asking God to come alongside you and teach you about this divinely powerful weapon. Ask Him to begin to train you and teach you how to destroy strongholds in your mind and heart. Ask Him to help you destroy arguments and pretentions about the knowledge of God. Ask Him to take your every thought captive to be obedient to Christ.

Your journey with your ex-spouse is an opportunity for God to teach you more and more about His nature, His desire for you, and His power to lead you deeper into His holiness. Trust Him to show you how to respond in meekness. When tempted to lash out at your ex-spouse, remember to trust God to lead you. Allow His Spirit to respond in meekness through you.

Day Two

Grace for the Thorn

While there are some stepfamilies who have great relationships with exes, more times than not, the ex-spouse becomes like an enemy to your newly blending family. While there is not ink and paper adequate to analyze the "why's", there are a number of solutions offered in God's Word.

Let me begin by saying that none of this is easy. In fact, everything I will present here is impossible. The challenge from yesterday's study may have felt impossible. But here is the encouragement. As a Christ-follower, you are indwelt with the Holy Spirit of God. The power of the resurrection of Christ was wrought by the Holy Spirit. The One who resides within you as the very presence of God Himself, is also imbued with the very **power** of God Himself. You are not called to live in a manner worthy of the Gospel of Christ in the power of the flesh. Instead, God has given you everything you need, through the Holy Spirit, to live the life He has called you to live.

God didn't say it would be easy, but He did say His grace is sufficient for us in our weakness. I know you remember the story of Paul's thorn in the flesh. That's where He really learned about the sufficiency of God's grace. We don't know what Paul's thorn actually was. But I have a feeling that sometimes your ex-spouse feels like a thorn in the flesh to you. If so, here's some additional encouragement, once again from our brother, Paul who lets us in on a personal conversation he had with God regarding his "thorn in the flesh."

Read 2 Corinthians 12:7-10.

What is the reason for Paul's thorn in the flesh?

What was the thorn?

How many times did Paul ask God to take away the thorn?

49

What was God's response?

Paul is considered the greatest missionary of all time. He had many amazing experiences throughout his life. He had a profoundly intimate relationship with God. Yet, Paul also suffered from a chronic ailment. Theologians have disagreed for years about the source of the thorn. But the honest answer is that no one knows for sure what tormented Paul. Probably because it wasn't important for us to understand the "what." The lesson for Paul, and for us, is when adversity comes, and thorns torment us, God may not deliver us. However, the incredible hope we have is through God Himself. While God does not deliver Paul from the thorn, He does promise the sufficiency of His grace to help Paul endure. The same sufficient grace is available to us as well.

Perhaps the primary lesson in the story is this. Even though the thorn remained, Paul had to continually rely on God's grace to endure. Paul certainly makes counter-culture declarations. While we westerners think strength is probably one of the greatest assets we can possess, Paul noted it was in his weakness that he boasted. Not a very popular stance in today's society, but I do think Paul was on to something important. Would I rather stand on whatever human strength I can muster on my own, or would I rather fall into the limitless depths of the strength of the Creator and Sustainer of the universe? I can be only as strong as my personal strength allows. But if I rely on God's strength, it is infinite in source and in power.

Why would God allow Paul to have a thorn in his flesh? Perhaps God was more interested in Paul's holiness than He was in Paul's comfort. Has God allowed a thorn in your flesh as well? I know many who would consider their ex-spouse as just such a thorn. There is great struggle and pain often at the hands of an ex-spouse. And the tables can also be turned. While we don't want to view it in the reverse, are you a thorn in the flesh of your ex-spouse? Depending on your perspective and your willingness to be completely honest with yourself, the thorn can go both ways.

Can you think of a time you acted as a thorn to your ex-spouse?

How would you have responded differently if given another opportunity?

What does God say about the thorn? Is He allowing your ex-spouse as a thorn in your life so that you can experience an infinite measure of His grace? As you allow the Holy Spirit to work in you and through you to endure the thorn, is He forming within you more of the character and nature of His Son? That is, after all, His goal for you … He longs for **all** of us to be conformed to the image of His Son.

In this text, Paul uses the word *sufficient, power* and *perfect*. Sufficient means God's grace is the only thing I need in order to experience the perfection of His power in my life. And sufficiency says that God supplies just the right amount of what I need, when I need it for any circumstance or situation. While I may feel the need to control or manipulate encounters with an ex-spouse, God says to allow His grace to meet whatever the need is and that He will do it powerfully and sufficiently.

Do you ever feel any competition with your ex-spouse? It may not be on the surface, but sometimes is there an underlying need to be better than they are? To have more money or a better house or for the kid's to prefer time with you over time with them? Do you want to take the kids on better vacations or provide a "more stable" environment? Human nature says these are all normal reactions and desires. But God says that the Spirit and flesh are warring with each other. While the human part of you wants to be "better" than your ex-spouse, the Spirit says to consider others as more important than yourself. Instead of demanding your own rights, meekness would respond by serving others. Instead of loving your friends and hating your enemies, meekness would say it's easy to love those who love you, but you are to love your enemies as well.

In God's desire to help you become conformed to the image of His Son, He has given you the Spirit to help you live differently than your flesh demands. He has given you the power to rise above and live a life which honors Him.

As we close today, consider the grace you have through Christ. Are you allowing the sufficiency of His grace to rule over your weakness? Perhaps grace is at the root of a spirit of meekness. Spend some time in prayer thanking God for the sufficiency of His grace. Pray, asking Him to help you to allow His grace to prompt you to respond in meekness.

Day Three

Loving Your Enemy

> *"You have heard that it was said, 'Love your neighbor and hate your enemy.' But I tell you: Love your enemies and pray for those who persecute you, that you may be sons of your Father in heaven. He causes his sun to rise on the evil and the good, and sends rain on the righteous and the unrighteous. If you love those who love you, what reward will you get? Are not even the tax collectors doing that? And if you greet only your brothers, what are you doing more than others? Do not even pagans do that? Be perfect, therefore, as our heavenly Father is perfect." Matthew 5:43-48*

It is a bitter irony that perhaps your ex-spouse has become your enemy. While you once had feelings of love and affection, you now find yourself as opponents on every field. Love, affection and kindness have perhaps turned to indifference, disdain and bitterness.

As difficult as it may be to admit, none of these feelings are born of the Spirit. While you may certainly have reason for these new feelings, none of them are God-honoring. So, what do you do with these feelings, and how to you turn the corner and begin to respond as Christ would?

🕮 *Read Matthew 5:43-48 again.*

What is the logical worldly advice with regard to enemies?

What does Jesus say about enemies that is completely counter-culture?

Think about what Jesus is really saying. He begins with the obvious. He states what the flesh would tell us. Love your neighbor and hate your enemy. I would assume He got some *amen's* to that. However in the very next breath, He turns a corner with *but*. One of Jesus' favorite sentence starters became "*but I tell you...*" As I read scripture, I always look for that, because it tells me Jesus is going to say something which sounds impossible or at least unrealistic. Such is the case here.

He takes what others would see as obvious and turns it around to get folks attention. While we can understand loving our neighbor and hating our enemy, He challenges us to think and respond differently. He tells us to love our enemies and pray for those who persecute us! Something tells me the previous *amen's* in his sermon suddenly fell silent.

While no one says it out loud, I'm sure everyone's thoughts are screaming, "Are you crazy? That's impossible! You don't know what my enemy has done to me and you don't have any idea of the depth of persecution I've experienced! There is **no way** I can do what you are suggesting!"

Is that how you feel about your ex-spouse? After all, they've done nothing but try to make your life miserable. They have treated you unfairly. They have betrayed you. They have deceived you and lied to you. And persecution? They have tried to turn your children against you. They have spoken hurtful and sometimes untrue words about you to your children. They have hired attorneys to destroy you before a judge and have asked crippling amounts of money from you for alimony or child support. Nothing is fair and you are the one who feels the most unfairly treated. After all, they are the one whose infidelity ended the marriage. You have tried time and again to work things out and have taken the brunt of the children's anger and hurt. Surely God wouldn't ask you to love them and pray for them.

But, remember, God doesn't do things the way the world does. His plan for us is that we be conformed to the image of His Son. So how did Jesus respond? One of His own "family" of followers betrayed Him. One of His own "family" of followers denied even knowing Him. His "family" scattered when things got tough. But how did Christ respond? Not only did He give His life for those who were His close friends and followers, but He also died for those who nailed His hands and feet to the cross. Then He asked His heavenly Father to forgive them.

The scenario I described above may not be accurate for you. There may have been other circumstances that ended your marriage. You may have been the one who was unfaithful. Some of the feelings I described may be more attributable to your ex-spouse than to you. But over time, many ex-spouse relationships dissolve into painful, hurtful exchanges where both parties behave much more as enemies than friends.

Here is the challenge. Spend the next seven days praying for your ex-spouse by name. And I'm not asking you to pray that God's vengeance would fall on them or that He would give them leprosy or financial ruin. I mean genuinely pray for God to be with them and speak to them. Ask Him to comfort their pain as they endure the grief of the loss of your family. Speak their name before the Father asking Him to help them through the day as He reveals Himself.

Secondly, when you hear of words they have spoken against you, resist the urge to retaliate or defend yourself. Stop at that moment and pray for them. Ask God to be your defender. Since this often happens with your children, ask God to help the children see the truth. And do not speak unkind words about your spouse to others. Try not to disrespect your ex-spouse to the children. Take the high road. Trust God to help your children see the truth.

Jesus teaches us the result of loving our enemy and praying for those who persecute us is that we may be sons of our Father in heaven. What does it mean to be a son of our Father in heaven? Be careful that you don't interpret this as salvation. Salvation is only obtained in one way. Jesus said, *"I am the way, the truth and the life. No one comes to the Father except through Me" (John 14:6)*. Jesus is declaring that He paid your sin debt on the Cross. Nothing you can do will ever earn your salvation. Jesus has paid the ransom for you and He offers salvation to you as a free gift. You can either accept the gift, or reject it.

Jesus is not saying if you love your enemy and pray for your persecutor that you will be saved. God is giving you the opportunity to grow in His grace. One of the ways you do so is by allowing His Spirit to mold you and make you more like Jesus. When you choose love over hate, you are choosing the way of Christ. You are allowing God to transform you on the inside to be more like Christ. When you pray for those who persecute you and speak evil against you, you are allowing God to deepen your compassion for them, allowing you to begin to see them the way God sees them.

God, in His sovereignty allows the sun to shine and the rain to fall upon the righteous and the unrighteous. While we don't understand this, we can trust God. He is working in both the righteous as well as the unrighteous to bring His plan to light in the lives of His children. God is at work among all people. He longs for all people to accept Christ's free gift of salvation. We must trust that His work is being accomplished even when we don't see or understand what God is up to.

In order for us to be salt and light (*Matthew 5:13-14*), we must look different than the world looks. We are called to be set apart in order that others can see Christ in us. When we love our enemies, the world notices. People loving someone who has caused them great pain. People forgiving someone of a heinous act. People showing kindness in unexpected ways. These are what cause people to stand up and take notice. I think that is what Jesus asks of us in this passage.

How you treat your ex-spouse has a huge impact on others, beginning with your own children. While the kids may be angry and bitter that you are no longer a nuclear family, they can learn a great deal about how to deal with adversity by watching how you choose to handle the relationship you now have with your ex-spouse. What character traits do you want to teach your children? Do you desire to teach them to become angry and bitter when life doesn't turn out how they want? Or do you want them to see trust and perseverance when life hands them difficulties? There will come a day when your children look back on the circumstances surrounding your divorce and relationship with your ex-spouse, and evaluate it through their own lens. While there are many things about the situation you cannot control, the one thing you have absolute control over is how you choose to respond.

Your children will someday understand and comprehend the pain you have suffered. They will also be able to process how you handled your pain. Did you rise above and live victoriously, seeking the best for your ex (who also happens to be their parent), or did you allow the circumstance to bury you and cause you to be vicious and malicious? Your children will be impacted by how you choose to live in the face of adversity. Regardless of how you have responded in the past, you can begin to respond differently today. What do you need to do differently in order to respond to your ex-spouse in meekness? Trust God to help you overcome any feelings which stand in the way.

Jesus chooses to end this portion of His discourse with a challenge that seems impossible. He tells us to be perfect just as God is perfect. We, as humans are unable to be perfect. However, the real meaning of the word perfect in this context is more akin to being complete or finished, pure and holy. It should always be the goal and desire of the Christ-follower to press on toward perfection, or completeness in grace. Paul reminds the Philippians *"He who began a good work in you will carry it on to completion until the day of Christ Jesus" (Philippians 1:6)*. He reminds them the goal is for this life to end complete, or having taken advantage of every opportunity to grow in faith and become more like Christ.

Thank you for persevering. I know these things are not easy to hear and even more difficult to implement in your life. But doing life God's way is always the best way. As you please and honor Him, you will grow deeper and deeper in your walk with Him. Spend some time in prayer. Allow the Holy Spirit to speak to your heart as you consider how you might better love your enemy.

Day Four

The Battle Belongs to the Lord

Today we are going to visit an Old Testament King whose name is Jehoshaphat. Although you may be wondering what an Old Testament king has to do with dealing with your ex-spouse and the beatitude of meekness, bear with me, and I promise, at the end of the day, this will all make sense.

Before we jump into the story of Jehoshaphat in *2 Chronicles*, let me give you a little bit of background. From the establishment of Israel as God's chosen people, there has been conflict. God laid out rules and guidelines for His people to live by. He originally established judges to help guide His people, because God Himself would be their king. Yet, the people were dissatisfied, and wanted an earthly king like their pagan neighbors. They were rebelling against the Theocracy God had established, and they longed for a Monarchy. God gave them what they wanted, and allowed them to replace the judges with kings. Then their troubles really began. Of the kings that ruled Israel, most were evil kings and led the people away from God. In fact, the kings actually divided Israel so that there was the northern kingdom called Israel whose capital was Samaria and the southern kingdom called Judah whose capital remained Jerusalem.

In the midst of the evil kings who ruled both kingdoms, there was an occasional bright spot. A king who followed God and led the people to walk in obedience. Jehoshaphat was just such a king. He was a king in Judah and was surrounded by nations who were the enemies of his country. Although Jehoshaphat's father, King Asa did not follow the Lord, *"the Lord was with Jehoshaphat because in his early years he walked in the ways his father David had followed. He did not consult the Baals but sought the God of his father and followed his commands rather than the practices of Israel." 2 Chronicles 17:3-4.*

"The Lord established the kingdom under his [Jehoshaphat's] control; and all Judah brought gifts to Jehoshaphat, so that he had great wealth and honor. His heart was devoted to the ways of the Lord; furthermore, he removed the high places and the Asherah poles from Judah." 2 Chronicles 17:5-6. The character of Jehoshaphat's heart would serve him well as we read the following encounter.

🔖 *Read 2 Chronicles 20:1-30*

Since *2 Chronicles 20:1* begins with an "after this", back up and read *2 Chronicles 19:4-11* to answer the question, "after what?"

Summarize what you learn about the heart of Jehoshaphat.

As we walk through this study of Jehoshaphat, ask yourself about your own heart when it comes to dealing with your enemies.

As chapter 20 opens, Jehoshaphat finds himself faced with attackers. As I read, the words "they started it!" resound in my mind. We found ourselves in just the same spot with an ex-spouse who, out of the blue, decided to take us to court. While it seemed everything was coming along just fine and we were "working together" to come to an agreement, the doorbell rang, and there was the court summons. Just like Jehoshaphat, we found ourselves surprised by an attack, and in need of a defense strategy.

When the report of his attackers came to Jehoshaphat, he found he was surrounded. There was no way out but to fight. Often times, when we are confronted with our enemies, we feel stuck. We are being attacked from all sides and it seems there is no earthly way to get out of the situation. We are forced to fight and come out swinging.

📖 *Read 2 Chronicles 20:3 again.*

What was Jehoshaphat's response to the news that his enemies were after him?

Jehoshaphat was alarmed. He was afraid and concerned and probably very anxious. He didn't really know what to do. So instead of panicking and calling all his military minds to come together and develop a battle strategy, he decided to inquire of the Lord. And he didn't just do it alone. He called the whole country to join him in seeking the Lord. What is your initial response when you know the enemy is on the warpath? Do you panic and begin to strategize? Do you get on the phone and start asking for advice? Or, do you stop and ask God what He wants you to do?

While your days of court appearances and visitation battles may be ancient history, there are still opportunities for conflict with an ex-spouse. There will always be family events where you will be together. No matter where you are in the journey with your ex-spouse, there is opportunity for growth in how you relate.

Let's get back to the people of Judah. As Jehoshaphat stood to address the people, he had an interesting speech for leading them against their enemies. He began by reminding the people of God's power. He recounted the times God had delivered His people in the past. He recognized God's sovereignty over all things, and affirmed his trust in God's deliverance.

He focused the attention of the people on God for deliverance, not the power and strength of his own army. He knew his army was too weak to defeat the vast armies that were coming against them. Only the power of God could save them from their enemies. He didn't seek the Lord for a plan; he simply sought the Lord.

Judah had been merciful to their neighbors as God had led them not to attack and take over the surrounding countries. Now, it seemed that their kindness and obedience to God was going to get them killed. They had not provoked their enemies to attack, yet found themselves surrounded by blood-thirsty enemies. They had only shown mercy. And now, they were the victims. Outnumbered and overpowered, they would surely be defeated.

I don't know if you can relate or not, but many conversations we have with blending families migrate to the topic of dealing with the struggles of an ex-spouse. You may have taken the high road and tried to show kindness and compassion. You may have been restrained in talking about your ex-spouse in front of your children. You may have tried to be amicable when it came to finances and visitation. But where did that get you? Perhaps today you feel as though all that was meaningless because your ex is now attacking you and trying to overpower you. You may find yourself in and out of courtrooms, spending thousands of dollars on attorneys who seem to be arguing over the most insignificant details. You may be struggling because you have lost control of how your kids are being raised in another household. You may feel as though you are being verbally attacked and accused of things that are not true.

In the midst of Judah seeking the Lord, He sent an answer through Jahaziel. God's Spirit spoke to the people and told them not to be afraid or discouraged because of the vast army that confronted them. Jahaziel proclaimed the battle was not theirs, but belonged to God.

Wherever you are with regard to your enemies, you can know that the battle you face is not yours, but His. As difficult as it is to believe, He longs to do a work in you. He longs to do a work in your family. God has a spiritual plan greater than the battle you face.

As the people of Judah sought the Lord, He brought them comfort and He brought them deliverance. For Judah, God's instructions were clear. He assured them they would not have to fight the battle. Instead, He told them to take up their positions, stand firm, and watch for His deliverance.

What is it that God is speaking to you with regard to your enemy? Is He telling you to trust Him with the battle? Is He asking you to stand firm and watch Him work? Is He asking you to pray for your enemy and show mercy and compassion?

There are two things that Jehoshaphat did after hearing God's plan. He bowed down and worshipped the God who delivers, and he had faith. The people of Judah didn't wait until it was all over to worship. In fact, they hadn't yet seen anything happen with their eyes. They only knew what God had said. Yet, they worshipped and believed God.

Has God spoken to you, but you are yet to see the fulfillment of His word to you? Perhaps the greatest lesson we can learn from Jehoshaphat is to worship God for who He is as much as what He does, and that our faith is what God is most interested in seeing. God may be waiting for you to worship Him before you see the fulfillment of His purpose amidst the attacks of your enemy. Perhaps He is growing your faith as you wait and trust. Maybe He desires that you remain close to Him as you endure.

You have read the end of Jehoshaphat's battle. You know God defeated the enemies of Judah. When they topped the hill, anticipating a battle, they saw only dead bodies. The battle was over before it ever started.

I know you must be thinking that this is a great story, but where is the practical application? Here are five things we can apply from the story of Jehoshaphat.

Take your enemy to God. When trouble comes and you are faced with a confrontation, take it to God. Talk to Him. Remember He is sovereign over even the most impossible struggles. Be conscious of the power of His Holy Spirit in you when encountering the conflict. Embrace His peace and compassion. Trust Him to control your anger.

Trust God to hear you. God is listening … not just to your words, but to your heart. Allow Him to comfort you and give you wisdom for how to deal with your enemy. Trust Him to know and do what is best for everyone.

Don't get discouraged. Let God have the battle. Release the confrontation to God. Let Him deal with it. One of the most difficult things to relinquish is control. But just let it go. God knows what's best for everyone involved in the battle. Remember, He is the God of redemption. He wants to redeem the people and circumstance. There are likely children who are watching, listening and learning. Teach them to trust God by showing them how, even in the most difficult battles.

Praise God and have faith. God inhabits the praises of His people. Allow Him to completely fill you as you praise. It is difficult to be upset when focusing on who God is. Allow your praise to deepen your faith. As you focus on Him, you will trust Him more deeply. As the people began to praise, their enemies were defeated. The truth is, your enemy isn't really your ex-spouse. **The enemy** wants to use any and all situations to bring division and strife. Don't allow him to do it. While there are many opportunities for anger and bitterness, allow God to defeat the enemy that longs to destroy you and your family. While you are no longer a nuclear family, God still desires that you grow in holiness. He still wants to do a work in you. You have an amazing opportunity to grow in new and sometimes miraculous ways.

Thank God for the victory. While you may not experience the same outcome as the people of Judah, focus on the victory that occurs each time you allow God to take over your thoughts and emotions. This story is not a guarantee that the court decision will always go your way, or you will always walk away feeling as though you have won the battle of the day, but it is a picture of God at work. Where He really gets the victory is in you. As you learn to trust Him in even the most difficult circumstances, you will know He is working in your heart. He is forming you into the likeness of His Son.

Your divorce is no surprise to God. While He may be heart-broken your family is now fractured, He knew you would be exactly where you are today. You can trust He has a plan for your family and your future. He also has a plan for your ex-spouse and their future. While your relationship with your ex-spouse has changed and will continue to change you can trust God with that relationship.

While restoring your family is no longer an option, He does desire that there be reconciliation of relationships. I don't know what form the reconciliation will take, but He longs for you to overcome the pain and bitterness that may surround your relationship with your ex-spouse.

Ask God to equip you and guide you as you seek to build a new relationship. Without a doubt, forgiveness is a cornerstone of anything that He builds. Pray for your ex-spouse. God desires to do a work in them as well. Trust Him as He rebuilds the lives of everyone who has been touched by the breakup of your family.

As you consider the best way to deal with an ex-spouse, keep your children in mind. I know that sounds obvious, but sometimes we become so embroiled in the battles, that we forget there are innocent casualties. While you and your ex-spouse have reasons for divorcing and no longer desire to be a nuclear family, your children don't. They still love both of their parents, and likely, their greatest desire is for their family to be reunited. As you become distracted by the crumbling relationship between the two of you, your children are being pelted with the debris. Remember that they see, hear and feel what you do. You may no longer love their mom or dad, but they do.

Let your children see you trust God when things are not fair. Let them see your faith grow as you encounter difficulties with your ex-spouse. Show them how to love unconditionally when your heart is tested. Let them see grace, mercy and meekness in action.

🐾 As we close our time together today, you may want to re-read the story of Jehoshaphat. There are many truths to glean. Do you have doubts about the battle you are facing right now? If so, write out those doubts.

What will it take to release your doubts to God?

Allow God to speak His truths to you, and trust Him with the battle.

Day Five

Godly Resolve

"You're blessed when you're content with just who you are – no more, no less. That's the moment you find yourselves proud owners of everything that can't be bought." Matthew 5:5 (The Message)

As we end this week's discussion on ex-spouses, let me encourage you. Of all the contacts we've made and all the interviews we've done, without question, dealing with an ex-spouse is the most difficult thing blending families face. Honestly, the same would likely be true for single parents as well. Especially if there are children, the issues encountered with the ex-spouse are at the top of the list of difficulties.

And a fairly recent issue we have encountered are couples who share a child, but never married. There are no legal decrees that founded the marriage nor dissolved it. The parents of the child don't have clear-cut guidelines under which to operate. There may or may not be financial support. There may or may not be regular visitation guidelines. But when one or both of the parents choose to marry another, the same complications occur as with an ex-spouse.

No doubt, the discussion this week has been difficult. For those of you who have figured out how to have an amicable relationship with your ex, I applaud you. As you experience this study in small group settings, I can only pray that there is a couple who can encourage the group through the success of an amicable "ex" relationship.

Bringing this discussion to a close, I want to end on a positive note. While you can't control what your ex-spouse does or doesn't do, you have an opportunity. God has a calling for your life. Regardless of the reason for your divorce, you now have the opportunity to experience and express redemption and Godliness.

I once read on a church marquee advertising a marriage retreat, a line that definitely captured my attention. It said something like, "perhaps God didn't give you your marriage to bring you happiness, but to help you develop holiness." Wow. That was quite a statement to ponder.

It made me rethink some of my motives for what I want out of my marriage. But really, if God gave me my marriage in order to make me holy instead of happy, my entire perspective on marriage could be transformed.

Perhaps you can view your relationship with your ex-spouse in the same way. While you would probably love to have a completely unified relationship with no snags along the way, where everyone is pleasant and kind, God may want to use your circumstance to teach you. Dealing with an ex-spouse is probably one of life's greatest challenges to Godliness.

God is not being metaphoric when He says a husband and wife become one. He does an amazing work with those two individuals, joining them together in a spiritual union. They are no longer two, but have become one flesh. He has bound them together.

When a marital union is dissolved, it is like tearing apart the flesh that has been joined. No matter the cause or reason for divorce, the broken union is more than just a legal document that changes the legal status of two people. There is a spiritual "tearing apart," separating the one back into two. Perhaps that's why it is often so difficult to develop a positive relationship with an ex-spouse.

But consider this. God has given you an opportunity to experience Godliness and holiness in one of life's most difficult relationships. He has given you the chance to experience the epitome of self**less**ness.

Before you begin today's study, spend some time in prayer. Ask God to completely open your heart to Himself. Ask Him to give you the courage to seek His holiness and Godliness as you deal with your ex-spouse. We will end our week in the Psalms.

🕮 *Read Psalm 37.*

Record everything the Psalmist says about the wicked.

You may have been tempted to picture your ex-spouse every time you read about the wicked. And yes, they may have caused you some grief and made life difficult. We all have stories about ex-spouses. But be careful in your attitudes. If there are evil motives or wicked deeds you have experienced at their hands, trust God with them. It is not for you to judge their motives, nor is it for you to seek revenge or justice. The Psalmist is very clear that God knows the hearts and motives and He is the One Who will handle the wicked. You have the opportunity to let go of any ill-will you have toward your ex-spouse, and trust God with them.

🕮 Now, record everything you are instructed to do in *Psalm 37.*

Record what you learn about those who **hope** in the LORD.

Record what you learn about the **meek**.

Record what you learn about the **blameless**.

Record what you learn about the **righteous**.

What do you learn in *Psalm 37:23*?

Record what God will do.

What does verse *Psalm 37:37* say about the man of peace?

This chapter is so full of what God desires and what He wants to do in the lives of those who are committed to follow in His ways. As you deal with the struggles and frustrations that may come with your ex-spouse, remember to focus most on what God wants to do in your own life. Focus on the list you made about the righteous. Look at what the Psalmist teaches about what "you" are to do and how you are to conduct yourself. Although it may be difficult to admit, there are two sides to divorce and the ex-spouse story. You not only have an ex-spouse, but you are an ex-spouse. Allow God to speak to your heart and bring to light anything that you have done or are doing to make life difficult for them.

The greatest peace I find in this passage has to do with letting go and trust. We read that we are not to fret. In fact, I read it three times in this passage. In order to not fret or be anxious, we have to trust God. All throughout this passage there is the assurance God has everything under control. He is dealing with the wicked, but He is also blessing the righteous.

As we close this week, spend some time meditating about the righteous. Are you righteous? Can you really look honestly at yourself and claim the promises of God for those who are righteous? Allow God to be brutally honest with you. God wants to do more in your life than simply making you feel as if justice has been served with regard to your ex-spouse. There will likely never be what you consider complete justice. But God longs to do a far greater work in you and in your family. Trust Him as you journey. Trust Him as you seek righteousness. Trust Him to guide you as you traverse the sometimes rough waters of dealing with an ex-spouse.

🔍 What are some issues with your ex-spouse that God has brought to mind as you have studied this week?

How is He challenging you to respond in meekness?

Consider creating an action plan to help you deal more positively with your ex-spouse. How can you be proactive to relate with them in a spirit of meekness?

"Be still before the Lord and wait patiently for Him; do not fret when men succeed in their ways, when they carry out their wicked schemes. Refrain from anger and turn from wrath; do not fret – it leads only to evil. For evil men will be cut off, but those who hope in the Lord will inherit the land." Psalm 37:7-9

Week Four

Hunger and Thirst

"Blessed are those who hunger and thirst for righteousness, for they will be filled." Matthew 5:6

Parenting is never easy. You would think we would be cruising through this season of life as four of our five children are now in their 20's. When everyone was at home and the schedules were insane and we spent all our time getting kids to and from activities and events, we sometimes dreamt of this season of life. During the heyday of having all the kids at home, we never knew how many mouths would show up for dinner. And usually there were more mouths than I had planned for! We lived crazy days of exhaustion and excitement, participating in everything we could as life revolved around our kids.

We would sometimes ponder what it would be like when the kids were no longer living at home. And now, here we are. Only, it isn't exactly as I thought it would be. There has never been a quiet, calm season at all. While we only have one still in middle school and all the others moving on with life, parenting hasn't really gotten any easier. It is just different now.

We have one who just recently married. Not only did our family grow by one more, but the newlyweds are trying to figure out where, what, when, how and why. We have another who has returned to us and is trying to figure out the same thing. One is on the other side of the world, and yes, trying to figure out what's next. The fourth is in college, so you know that journey. While we may have thought we would be finished parenting by now, it feels like parenting is even more intense now than when the kids were young. The stakes are higher. Consequences are more life-altering. Choices have deeper, longer-lasting, more expensive outcomes. The future is uncertain. There isn't an assurance of the "next grade" coming in the fall. They have to figure out how to make ends meet when next fall comes.

I have probably just lost all the readers who still have children at home. You have decided this is all too discouraging and you just want to quit now. But please hang in there. Although the way you parent changes as your children grow, your parenting role is life-long. No matter their age, you still have a place, a voice and a purpose in the lives of your children.

I do have one golden nugget of truth when it comes to parenting. I know you can't wait to hear "the secret" to parenting. I can even say, this is the key to step-parenting as well.

Ready? Anxious to hear? Here is the secret to parenting. God wants to do as much *in* me as the parent as He wants to do *through* me to impact my children.

That may not sound like much to you, but to me it was a profound epiphany. I had always thought of parenting as solely focused on my children. God wanted to use me to impact the lives of those He had placed in my home and entrusted me to raise. But the further along I go in this parenting and step-parenting journey, the more I understand that God is doing a sometimes greater work in me than He's doing through me. We are all on a journey, no matter our age. While you may feel the weight of parenting heavy on your shoulders, know that you have Someone who is there to carry the burden of it all, because He longs to do a work in you as well.

I hope this week's study will encourage you as you build your new family. No matter where you are on the road as a blending family, perhaps there will be nuggets of truth and encouragement to help you along the path. Enjoy the focus of the week. Are you hungry and thirsty, running on empty, longing to be filled? As we study *"Blessed are they that hunger and thirst for righteousness, for they will be filled,"* let God take you and teach you about what it means to let Him take over and fill you to overflowing!

Day One

What is the Source?

Before we begin our journey into this beatitude, I want us to do a little background and understand just where our provision comes from. The fact that Jesus uses the metaphor of hunger and thirst in this beatitude, tells us that what He shares has to do with basic need. Without food and water, we will perish. But Jesus' intent in this beatitude is to help us understand that just as food and water are essential to our physical survival, so righteousness is essential to our spiritual survival.

Practically, you may feel overwhelmed caring for your new, larger family. You may even have financial obligations to another household where your children now reside. But realizing the source of even the physical provision, might help encourage you as you begin to consider what Jesus is preaching when He discusses righteousness.

When we consider our own need for righteousness, we may feel overwhelmed as well. I don't know about you, but I feel like a mess much of the time. I can't seem to control my tongue, my anger takes over, I have thoughts I know I should not have. When it comes to stepchildren, we all may find ourselves feeling overwhelmed and completely out of our league. How in the world can I manage this new household righteously?

When Jesus said that we should hunger and thirst after righteousness, He seemed to institute a sense of urgency or deep longing. As important as bread and water is to our physical life, so righteousness is to our soul. When we find ourselves hungry and thirsty to live a righteous life, we are not alone. Throughout scripture, men and women have been challenged with the same. Let's look into the Old Testament to see a picture of the One Who provides the righteousness that is life to our soul.

In the Old Testament, God would be called different names, based upon the nature or character that was revealed to a specific person in a specific situation. One of the names used for God, is *El-Shaddai*. The Hebrew meaning of this name is *All-Sufficient One*. God had a number of names in the Old Testament that began with El followed by another descriptor. The Hebrew word El can be best translated as God. Many times the name *El-Shaddai* is translated as God Almighty. The exact meaning of *Shaddai* is not clear. However, looking at some of the Hebrew root words gives us a picture of the intent of this title for God.

Some of the words that describe *Shaddai* include provision and blessing. The word also indicates that God is the One who nourishes and satisfies our needs. Part of this word can be linked to the Hebrew word for "breast," with the implication of sustaining, as a mother who is the lifeline to her nursing child. Another root word that can help us better understand this name of God is the Hebrew *shadad* which means to overpower or destroy. So, when combining all these Hebrew root words, we understand that God is the One who nourishes, blesses and is all-powerful to protect and sustain. Finding a single descriptor that would communicate the incredible power and unlimited provision of God would require more than one word. Simply the fact that a number of similar Hebrew words were used to construct this idea tells of the unfathomable depths of God's All-Sufficiency.

When we see the first occurrence of a new name of God, it is important that we understand the context. Seeing how God first used this name as He interacted with His people will give us insight into the meaning as well.

🕮 Read Genesis 17:1-8.

In *Genesis 17:1*, the *New American Standard* translation tells us that God appeared to Abram and said, "I am God Almighty." This is El-Shaddai.

How old was Abram when He encountered God in this passage?

What is God's message to Abram?

What happens to Abram during this encounter?

During this exchange between God and Abram, God reveals to Abram that He is going to multiply Abram's descendants exceedingly. Remember, time had passed since the Abrahamic Covenant was established in *Genesis 15,* and Hagar had given birth to Ishmael some eleven years earlier. Actually, 24 years had elapsed since God first told Abram of the promised offspring (*Genesis 12:4*).

By the time God goes to Abram in *Genesis 17,* Abram could have very well just given up on the promise. Perhaps this is a good time to chase a rabbit. When we read stories in the Bible, we already know the end of the story. But stand for just a minute in the sandals of Abram and Sarai. What God promised and what they saw seemed completely at odds. Sarai was barren to begin with. How much more barren would she be as an old woman some 25 years later?

Think for a moment about your own life. Do you remember times when you know God has spoken, yet you look around at your circumstances and doubt Him? Perhaps you have been praying for reconciliation with a family member and it seems to be impossible. You may be praying for a child who is far away from God and you've waited so long to see them return to faith in Him. It might be that the promise you have from God about the hope and joy you would find in the new family He gave seems so fraught with obstacles that you can't imagine anything beyond the conflict and struggle you find yourself in.

Abram and Sarai had seemingly given up on God. But even though they doubted, God showed up. He reminded Abram of the promise He made so many years ago. I see the faithlessness of this couple in how they sought to make God's will happen on their own. Sarai grew so impatient in waiting on God to give Abram a son, that she took matters into her own hands. Instead of waiting on God, she arranged for her handmaiden, Hagar, to give Abram a son. But that wasn't God's plan.

But lest you think Sarai was the only one who took God's plans into her own hands, consider what Abram had to say. In *Genesis 15:2*, Abram doubted God. He knew God had a plan for an heir. But in Abram's temporal way of thinking, because he and Sarai were old and barren, God surely must intend for his inheritance to go to his faithful servant Eliezer. How difficult it is for us to just believe God and trust Him to do what only He can do. I don't know about you, but when God speaks to me, my first temptation is to begin to figure out how I can make it work.

🐾 What do you do when it seems like God is not following through on a promise He has made?

How do you wait?

I think perhaps God wanted to use the 24 years between promise and fulfillment to help prepare Abram and Sarai for what He would do through them. Maybe God is preparing you as well. Maybe there are other circumstances not yet in place. God's timing is never our timing. God's timing is always perfect.

I encourage you today, whatever it is you are waiting on God to do in your life, a promise that is unfulfilled, wait in faith and trust God as the ultimate promise-keeper. We have a bit of insight that Abram and Sarai lacked. We have the complete revelation of God in scripture. *Hebrews 11:1* gives us instructions for how we are to wait. This passage tells us to wait in faith. *"Now faith is the assurance of things hoped for, the conviction of things not seen." Hebrews 11:1*

The meaning of assurance of things hoped for implies a confidence in your waiting. You are waiting expectantly based on God's faithfulness and power. So, the next time you are tempted to give up on God, remember that He never stops working and His promises are always yes, and amen. Now back to Abram and *Genesis 17*.

🔖 What does God do in *Genesis 17:5*?

It is interesting that God sometimes changes the names of His people. In the Eastern culture, this is done to signal a new circumstance in history for the individual. Interestingly, God also changes Sarai's name to Sarah in *Genesis 17:15*. The name Abram means *high father*, but when God changed the name to Abraham, the meaning of the name changed to *father of many or multitudes*. God changes the names to confirm to the couple that He is faithful to bring about that which He had promised.

So what does this have to do with our beatitude? Jesus compels His listeners to hunger and thirst after righteousness, for they will be filled. While the analogy of bread and water bring to mind the most basic of needs, Jesus wants us to know that God is All-Sufficient. Our righteousness is not found in our own attempts to provide sustenance for ourselves. Our only hope for righteousness comes through Him. Tomorrow we will go deeper into Jesus' challenge that we hunger and thirst for righteousness.

I hope the lesson today has given you much to consider. As you close your time of study, consider a time when you feel like God has let you down, or hasn't come through for you. It may be in your personal life or in the life of your family. Go to Him and share your heart. Tell Him your struggles. Then, be silent and listen. Is He leading you to a particular scripture passage to help encourage you? Has He given you a word of encouragement through another believer along the way? Let God give you rest and peace as you wait on Him to do what He's promised in your life.

This week we will hopefully gain some insight into parenting and step-parenting. As you spend time in God's Word, I hope you will look at the study as an opportunity to grow in your skills. Blessed are those who hunger and thirst for righteousness … as a step-parent, you will likely find yourself in times of dilemma. What are you hungering and thirsting after in those moments? Do you allow God's righteousness to guide you? In moments of frustration or indecision about how to handle a situation, look to God. Your El-Shaddai has everything you need to parent His way. Trust Him as your All-Sufficient One.

Day Two

Hunger for Righteousness

Yesterday, we looked at the One providing for us. We also contemplated the deep need each of us have that we cannot fill on our own. As we consider the blessed who hunger and thirst for righteousness, we need to understand more in depth, what Jesus is saying. Let's break this down. There are three things we must understand to fully fathom the weight of this passage. First, what does it mean to hunger and thirst for *righteousness*?

The term righteousness as used in the New Testament has two implications. One implication is borne out of the Hebrew Old Testament which explains righteousness in terms of God's covenantal relationship with Israel. The New Testament Greek meaning expands righteousness to define living life within the confines of the law. Obviously, this is the reason we need a Savior. No one is able to live a completely righteous life.

In practical terms, righteousness is not so much "being good" but living out God's will through obedience and reliance upon Him for our moment-by-moment journey through life. The idea of righteousness is two-fold. There is the verb which talks in terms of justice. We are made "just" before a Holy God. The only way we can be "just" before God is through the salvation of Christ. In that way, we exchange our sinful cloak for His garment of justification. We are no longer bound and controlled by our sin nature, but now are made "just" by the blood of Christ on the cross. The other side of the coin involves our living rightly before God. While our justification is secure, how we live out our commitment may or may not be consistent. Our desire should be to live as God has required, empowered by the Holy Spirit to walk out a life of "right living" ... choosing to live in accordance with God's Word.

I Am the Bread of Life

I'm sure you all remember the story, even if from childhood, of Jesus feeding the five thousand. While thousands had gathered to hear Him teach, the hour became late, the throngs were hungry and the food court at the mall did not deliver. The disciples came to Jesus in a bit of a panic, worrying that the hungry mob might become riotous. Wringing their hands, knowing they didn't have room on their credit cards to feed so many people even if they could find a caterer on such short notice, they turned to Jesus. How were they going to provide something to eat for so many? And even if they dismissed the crowd, there was nowhere for them to go for food. But, as luck would have it, a young boy with a mother of forethought had brought a snack with him. While the happy meal only contained two small fish and five loaves (probably more like biscuits), Jesus used it to solve the problem and teach an object lesson.

The story tells us that *"Jesus took the loaves, gave thanks, and distributed to those who were seated as much as they wanted. He did the same with the fish. When they had all had enough to eat, he said to his disciples, 'Gather the pieces that are left over. Let nothing be wasted.' So they gathered them and filled twelve baskets with the pieces of the five barley loaves left over by those who had eaten."*

While there is much to learn from this passage, I want to focus on the disciples. What had the disciples experienced in this situation? They observed Jesus take what they had, give thanks for it, and multiply it, having more than enough to feed the throngs. Jesus had originally intended to get away with just Himself and the disciples, but people followed. While He taught and blessed the people, the real lesson was for His closest followers. After everyone ate, there were 12 basketfuls left over ... one for each of the 12 disciples. The lesson for them? Not only would Jesus work through them to bless others, but He would also take care of their needs in miraculous ways.

Your task as a parent and step-parent might sometimes feel as impossible as feeding five thousand with a couple of fish and a few biscuits. You may be overwhelmed. But remember what God can do through you. The disciples were not expected to make the miracle happen. They simply followed Jesus' instruction. Imagine their surprise as the food seemed to multiply. As you are confronted with difficult situations and overwhelming feelings, God does not expect you to handle any of it alone. He is there. He is providing the wisdom and strength you need. He has all the grace and courage right there, in your hand. Trust Him. Hunger and thirst for Him to lead you and provide for your righteous responses and attitudes as you deal with difficulties.

📖 *Read John 6:25-35.*

Record every mention of bread.

Jesus speaks of the physical sustenance which is a temporal expression of that which He wants to provide for eternity. Bread the body consumes is not a lasting sustenance. For an everlasting life, one must partake of the eternal bread. In trying to understand what Jesus has just said, the disciples ask for a miraculous sign to help them believe. They refer to the miracle of the manna in the desert that their forefathers experienced. Jesus connects the miraculous manna-bread God gave them in the desert that sustained them physically, with the spiritual bread God sent in the form of Jesus. Where the manna sustained for a day, the Bread of Life in Christ will sustain through all eternity. When they asked for some of the bread Jesus described, Jesus identified Himself as the Bread of Life.

In the middle of this explanation of bread, there is a parenthesis that doesn't seem to fit. However, this is the center point of the exchange. These Jewish disciples had been taught the Jewish ways. They had grown up under the law, which demanded that they keep the law in order to be made righteous. Their question in *John 6:28* gives us a glimpse into the theology they had been raised on. *"What must we do to do the works God requires?"* They are trying to understand how to be made righteous. They had grown up understanding that righteousness was a result of their works.

Jesus had an unusual reply as a Rabbi. *"The work of God is this: to believe in the One he has sent."* I can just see the disciples looking at each other and at Jesus with quizzical expressions. They are trying to get their heads around this profound shift in thinking. Now let's return to the conversation about bread.

The disciples are trying to understand what it will take for them to have eternal life. Jesus is telling them it isn't works that will earn them salvation, but that they simply believe in the One who was sent. This is not a new idea. When God spoke to Abraham and promised that his descendants would be as numerous as the stars in the heavens, *"Abram **believed** the Lord, and he credited it to him as righteousness" (Genesis 15:6).* So righteousness that would come through a Messiah and not as a result of works was God's plan.

This is a good time to pause and consider another name for God. Jeremiah the prophet had a tough task. During his term as prophet, Israel had already fallen into exile, and Judah was well on its way. He preached a message of destruction, but also of restoration. Jeremiah is sometimes called the weeping prophet because he longed for God's people to return to faithfully living out God's plan for them. However, in the midst of Jeremiah's laments, he is able to contrast what the Jewish religious leaders are not doing with what God desires for His people. God says that His people are not keeping the covenant they made with Him. Their shepherds are teaching them that righteousness is based on works.

📖 *Read Jeremiah 23:1-6.*

What does Jeremiah say about the shepherds that are tending God's flock?

Who is going to step in?

What does *Jeremiah 23:5* tell us?

What is His name?

God introduces the Righteousness we cannot earn on our own. He tells His people there will come One who will be their Righteousness. In fact, He will be the righteousness for all mankind. In case you want to know, that name in Hebrew is actually *Jehovah-Tsidkenu*, The Lord our Righteousness. The coming Messiah would become righteousness on our behalf. As you can imagine, this did not sit too well with the Jewish religious leaders.

The Pharisees had distorted God's original plan and made righteousness something to be earned through actions. When Jesus told the disciples that their belief was enough, they asked for a sign. Isn't it interesting their example of a sign for their forefathers was the manna God send from heaven to feed them in the desert? While the children of Israel were hungry for physical bread, God miraculously fed them with bread from heaven that fell every day. He met their physical need to be sustained, while His heart longed for them to know Him as their sustenance for eternity. Jesus reminded the disciples that God had now sent a true bread from heaven. He explains that this true bread is *"he who comes down from heaven and gives life to the world" (John 6:33)*.

Still, the disciples don't seem to get it. They ask again how they can get this "bread." Jesus patiently spells it out for them. There are a couple of significant pieces to the statement Jesus makes in *John 6:35*. He says, *"I am the Bread of Life."* The fact that He uses the *I am* statement is intentional. Remember in the Old Testament when God calls to Moses out of the burning bush and tells Moses that he is going to deliver Israel out of the hands of the Egyptians? Moses is feeling inadequate and insecure, to say the least, and asks God about the certain questions of the people. Moses asks God what he is to say when the doubting Israelites ask Moses who has sent him to deliver them. God's answer? *"Tell them the I AM has sent you."* That term *I AM* is significant. It means *Self-Existent One.* In other words, there is no need for any other, because the *I AM* is sufficient. So when Jesus says *I AM the Bread of Life*, He is identifying Himself with God the Father. Just as God is Self-Existent and needs no other, so Christ is Self-Existent and needs no other to bring righteousness to man. Jesus is all the Bread we need to be sustained for all eternity. He closes by stating that *"He who comes to me will never go hungry, and he who believes in me will never be thirsty" (John 6:35)*.

We have traveled many miles in God's Word today. Let's try to bring everything together to see how what we have talked about connects with hungering and thirsting for righteousness as a step-parent.

Today we saw that righteousness is not possible "in the flesh." We are not able to live righteously in our own strength. However, we have One who walks beside us and provides complete righteousness. I suppose the question to ask is this: are you step-parenting like the Pharisees? They lived a life of rules and regulations. Their righteousness was external.

They were able to act righteously, yet their heart was completely focused on themselves. They were so busy "keeping up appearances" they had little interest in allowing God to do a work in their hearts.

Step-parenting requires us to take one more step beyond our biological parenting. Parenting in a nuclear family usually comes with less baggage. The love of two people comes together and produces a life. Together. As I write this, I am remembering the birth of my eldest. Today is his birthday. And this year the day and date coincide as they did on his actual birthday. It is Saturday and he was born on Saturday. I am fondly remembering everything I did on this most special day. There was nothing but joy and excitement as his dad and I considered adding another person to our family. There were no difficult feelings to overcome or resentment to resolve. Just joy and anticipation of a lifelong relationship with this precious new life.

However, when we gain someone else's children through marriage, we also gain the hurts and struggles that surround the new union. These children are older and have already established patterns we had nothing to do with. They are old enough to know whether they would choose us or not. There is no blood relationship tying us together. Everyone in the relationship chooses how they feel about the people suddenly thrust into their life. Step-parenting with righteousness challenges us. Here are some things to consider.

Godly righteousness requires a change of heart. You can "act" all day long, but when it comes down to it, your stepchildren know how you feel about them. While some of you may have instantly fallen in love with your stepchildren, others of you may have struggled with some of those relationships. Step-parenting righteously challenges us to go to God for a change of heart. Spend time in prayer asking Him to grow love in your heart for all your stepchildren, no matter how difficult they may be for you.

Step-parenting God's way is a partnership. I know you think I mean a partnership with your spouse. But in this case, you are challenged to partner with God as you step-parent. Step-parenting sometimes requires different responses than parenting your biological children. Godly wisdom is your greatest ally. You will find yourself in situations where you are genuinely at a loss. Parenting seems very intuitive. You generally just know what to do. But step-parenting is not usually so intuitive. However, if you will allow God to parent with you, He will give you just what you need for each situation.

God has a purpose for *you* in the life of your stepchildren. God did not give you your stepchildren by birth. However, He did give them to you. Trust that He has a plan for you in their life. While you may not be required to parent in the same way your spouse does, you do have a purpose in their life. Pray for your stepchildren. Ask God about the role He has planned for you in their life. Perhaps you are to model what it means to hunger and thirst after righteousness. You have the opportunity to be a neutral bystander in the relationship with your stepchildren that your spouse can't. The breakup of their family is not about you. You get to develop a relationship with your stepchildren outside of the hurt and pain of the breakup of their biological family. Hungering and thirsting after righteousness requires that you seek God's righteousness in step-parenting as if you were dying of hunger and thirst. Let God do a work in your relationship with your stepchildren.

There is much to consider from today's lesson. As we close for the day, consider what it means for you to hunger and thirst for righteousness. Are you allowing the Bread of Life to sustain you? Are you trusting God to be your righteousness? Spend some time in prayer. Meditate on what it means to truly hunger for righteousness.

Day Three

I Am the Living Water

Have you ever been parched? I mean really, really thirsty. In-the-desert-with-no-water thirsty. Likely, few of us have ever experienced the kind of thirst from which you almost perish. But we can probably all relate to needing a drink of water so bad that we obsess about it.

I think the analogy Jesus used of thirsting after righteousness carried with it just that much passion. While we may find ourselves a little bit in need of a drink, few of us really approach righteousness with the fervor of being parched almost to death.

As we look at the passage of scripture where Jesus identifies Himself as the Living Water, I want you to think about what it means to long for a drink of righteousness with the same urgency as needing a cup of water in the middle of the desert.

Read John 4:1-26.

What does Jesus do in *John 4:7*?

Why do you think He asked her this?

What was her response?

How did Jesus answer her response?

In this story, Jesus does so much to teach us about what living out our righteousness looks like. In the way of background, Jesus actually went out of His way to go through Samaria. The irony is that most Jews would go out of their way to stay out of Samaria. It was reviled and disgusting to Jews to even enter the town. Their disdain for Samaritans was great. And Jesus encountered a woman. The amazing thing here is that He actually

77

struck up a conversation. Jewish men would never value a Samaritan woman enough to even acknowledge her, much less engage in a dialogue.

Jesus took full advantage of the situation in order to share the truth of the Living Water with a woman who couldn't even come to draw water when the others were at the well. She was likely despised even by her own people because of her lifestyle. She came to the well in the heat of the day when she knew she wouldn't have to endure the town gossip. Yet Jesus valued her by asking for a drink, opening the conversation where He could share Himself as the Living Water.

What I appreciate about this story is that Jesus came to her, she did not come to Him. And he approached her in her sin. She admitted to having multiple husbands and even currently was living with a man not her husband. While law said she should have been stoned for her sinful lifestyle, Jesus saw within her the potential to be a follower of His. He saw her potential for redemption. He saw her need for His saving grace in her life.

When the parched life meets the Living Water, there is an amazing transformation. What once was dead and hopeless, now has a refreshing opportunity to choose life and hope. This woman was not only redeemed eternally, but Jesus gave her the chance to live a new life on earth, cleansed of her sin, forgiven and able to choose to live in obedience. We don't really know the end of her story beyond the fact she was changed after having encountered Jesus that day.

🔖 *Read John 4:39-42.*

This whole community was transformed because of one sinful woman's encounter with the Savior. She simply shared with others what Jesus had done for her. How does God want to use you to transform the lives of others? This woman was living in sin that was worthy of death, yet after she encountered Jesus, she was completely changed. Every time we are spiritually parched, The Living Water desires to do the same in us, too.

So back to *Matthew 5:6*. What is the result of your hunger and thirst for righteousness? Jesus says that you will be filled. I don't think He intends for you to just have a few drops or crumbs to hold you over until the real meal shows up. I think what He means is that when you really do long to live in righteousness, **He** will be the one to fill you up to the top. Perhaps you can even be filled to overflowing. As He satisfies you, the excess will spill over onto others. Your children experience a renewal of your righteousness living. Certainly your spouse will be blessed as you choose to live in righteousness. And even your ex-spouse will likely see a difference as your righteousness overflows even over them.

We have talked about how your own righteousness can impact the way you step-parent. Your hungering and thirsting for God's righteousness will equip you to live out His example in front of your spouse and stepchildren. But today, I want you to consider taking the righteousness one step further.

In the story we read today, when the woman encountered The Living Water, her life was so transformed that she affected others. Consider the impact your personal desire for righteousness can have on your family. The power of the righteousness of God is bigger than you are. As you live out your righteousness, those in your household will be influenced.

🐾 What does righteousness mean to you?

What is one thing you can do today to help you live out righteousness as a step-parent?

What will be your greatest obstacle?

Pray. Ask God to help you better understand His righteousness. Trust Him to continue to do a work in your heart. Ask Him to empower you to live righteously in your family.

Day Four

How's Your Appetite?

"You're blessed when you've worked up a good appetite for God. He's food and drink in the best meal you'll ever eat." Matthew 5:6 (The Message)

I hope the past three days' lessons have encouraged and inspired you to seek the righteousness of Christ in your life. Not only does seeking righteousness apply personally, but can also be an opportunity for your family. Many of us live our lives running on empty. That applies to every area of life. We experience emptiness emotionally and physically. Our relationships may feel empty and hollow. We certainly can feel spiritually drained. But is that the best way to experience the abundant life Christ offers?

We have seen how Christ is the bread of life and living water we need to experience a righteous life. But what does this have to do with our day-to-day experiences with work, life, and family? Your blending family may leave you feeling overwhelmed and drained much of the time. How can you really manage all the relationships and issues, the hurt and brokenness that has brought you together?

The bottom line is that as a family, and as a couple you must rely on the power and strength of Christ to sustain and fill you. The demands of any family are great, and God never intended for us to survive in our own strength. He longs to be everything we need in order to thrive as a family. We find even more demanding circumstances in a blending family. So how much more we need to rely on the power of the Holy Spirit in our lives to be able to thrive as a blending family.

Today, we are going to cover some very practical issues when it comes to growing as a blending family. While we have discussed some of the struggles to overcome, today I want us to focus on some things that will actually help strengthen your family. I want to shift the focus. Let's consider what it will take for your family to thrive instead of merely survive.

One of the major tenants of the nation of Israel had to do with their faith and passing that faith on to future generations. We have discussed the absence of obvious blending families throughout the Old Testament. However, you don't have to read very far to find lots of issues within families because they had not followed God's plan for family. As blending families we certainly don't need any help with regret and guilt over the past. We, better than most, understand God's desire for boundaries when it comes to family. Every day we deal with the consequences of a marriage that ended and family that is torn apart. Today, let's turn our focus away from the past and look to the present.

I know these words are trite, but can provide a great new perspective. *"Today is the first day of the rest of your life."* If we could all live by these words, we would experience freedom from the burden of the past. Wouldn't it be great if we could see the past through the lens of growth? Instead of regrets, why can't we view the past (mistakes and all) as an opportunity for growth, rather than an albatross of defeat?

So, for right now, we are going to consider today the first day of the rest of your life. You can't change yesterday or last year, but you can decide for this day, *"whom you will serve" (Joshua 24:15)*. So begin fresh today. Let's look at God's encouragement to His people.

🎀 *Read Deuteronomy 6:4-12.*

Record anything in this passage that could be considered a command.

You may recognize part of this as the Shema, the central prayer in the Jewish prayer book. In fact, *Deuteronomy 6:4-5* was so important to the Israelites that they recited this often. But like many other principles God gave them, the Shema became nothing more than a heartless recitation. They forgot that God's intent was to turn their hearts toward Him. The words became mere ritual. The Israelites came to rely on words to make them righteous, instead of allowing the words to transform their hearts. Let's look at what God really intended by this passage and the practical application for today's families.

First of all, God wants us to remember that He is the One True God. There is none other. Secondly, He wants us to understand His desire for our personal relationship with Him. He says that we are to love Him with **all** of our heart, **all** of our soul, and **all** of our strength. There is no room for anything or anyone else to occupy our devotion. Jesus reiterated this when He identified the greatest commandment. He went on to teach that our responsibility is to seek **first** His kingdom and righteousness. If we will do this, He will add everything else.

Lest we take this out of context, Jesus teaches this principle on the heels of telling His listeners they need not worry about life or provision. When we keep God at the forefront of life, all the things that would otherwise preoccupy our minds with worry and anxiety will be taken care of by our loving heavenly Father.

By the way, this is a great principle in blending families. While you may be overwhelmed and feeling completely ill-equipped to care for this new bunch of folks, Jesus says it plainly. You focus on seeking God, and He is faithful to take care of the rest.

🎀 *Read Matthew 6:25-34.*

Jesus wants us to give ourselves and our family to God. There are so many things we could worry about. But Jesus says God wants us to focus on Him and trust Him to take care of everything. I know Jesus is talking about physical provision in this passage, and perhaps that's not something you spend a lot of time worrying about. You have food, clothing and a place to live. Perhaps you are more preoccupied with the personal and relational struggles in your home. God wants these things as well. We sometimes don't have solutions for many of the issues we face in our home. But God has all the answers. We simply need to look to Him for not only provision, but for wisdom.

Matthew 6:33 says that we are to seek **first** the kingdom of God. The first principle we can apply is the order in which we seek. Do you go to God at the beginning of a problem or issue, or is He a last resort? You've tried everything else and nothing else works, so as a last resort, you go to Him in prayer. And is your heart really expecting Him to answer? Do you reluctantly go to God and half-heartedly ask? Remember the Shema? Remember the greatest commandment? We don't go to God *half*-heartedly. He asks that we come with our *whole* heart. He wants all your trust. He wants all your faith. He doesn't want your solution *and* Him. He wants you to trust Him alone. Wholeheartedly.

What exactly does Jesus mean when He talks about seeking the kingdom of God? In this passage, I believe Jesus refers to the Gospel. That is the power of the Holy Spirit being free to live out the Christ-life through the life of the believer. Certainly, in the flesh, we are powerless to overcome sin and live in victory. We are also unable to really provide fully for ourselves or for those over whom we are given charge. But the indwelling Holy Spirit is all-powerful. It is Christ in us who gives us the strength and wisdom to overcome the bondage of sin. He also provides the wisdom and courage to live the life God desires for us.

Along with seeking the kingdom of God, Jesus encourages us to seek His righteousness. While we discussed this earlier in the week, here we have another reminder that God desires we live out His plan for us. By living righteously we are freeing the Holy Spirit to work in and through us to bless the lives of others. Jesus doesn't want us to be divided in our heart by allowing the things of this life to choke out the freedom we have when living in the power and provision of God.

Back to the passage in Deuteronomy. God has an instruction for families as well. He has provided the basic truth for every person; that we are to love the Lord our God with **all** our heart, soul and strength. But that doesn't just go for us as individuals. As families, and parents in particular, we have a responsibility to teach this principle to our children.

I think God is anticipating that we might take this command and turn it into some sort of family catechism where we teach courses for our children to learn. God says this principle is to be on the *hearts* of children. We are to *impress* this on our children. Have you heard the phrase "caught more than taught?" I think that's exactly what God means here. This principle of whole-hearted devotion to the One True God is a way of life rather than a long list of rules to be followed. I think that's why He talks in terms of teaching about these things as you are living life. It isn't that we sit down and have classes for our children as much as we help them see how the principle is lived out in the daily-ness of life.

So what do your children see as you are living out your life? Do they see parents who are whole-heartedly devoted to the One True God? Do they see a family who is completely sold out to following the path God has laid out? Consider carefully the principles you are teaching your children. As they watch do they see you hungering and thirsting after righteousness? Or do they observe you making decisions that are rooted in selfishness? Do you respond with a heart turned toward God or with attitudes of the flesh?

As we close our time together today, spend time in prayer. Perhaps you and your mate would spend some time together in prayer. Then, discuss some things you might want to change in order for your family to seek God wholeheartedly. Pray especially for any relationships that are strained. Trust God to guide you in handling those relationships with righteousness.

Journal your thoughts of what God is teaching you.

Day Five

Filled for a Family Who THRIVES

As we close out this week, I want to focus on what it means to be filled. After all, this beatitude tells us that *"Blessed are they that hunger and thirst for righteousness, for they will be **filled**."* What does it mean to be filled? I think in this verse, Jesus is saying that we are filled with what we seek after. We can seek after many things, but only the things of God are truly satisfying. So how does God want to fill us?

We are going to spend today a bit differently as we study. I want you to have an opportunity to really focus on the things of God. I want you to consider how He will fill you when you earnestly seek after Him. We talked about *Matthew 6:33: "Seek first the kingdom of God and His righteousness and **all these things** will be added to you."* What are all these things?

Remember yesterday, you were challenged to help your family thrive? Survival is one thing, but the ability to really thrive brings living to a whole new level. As you connect God's filling with His desire that your family thrive, look at *Psalm 107.*

📖 *Read Psalm 107.*

I encourage you to really look at the Word and allow God to use it to speak to your heart. This passage talks about a journey of sorts where people experience life, their choices, and their circumstances. Then they encounter the power and presence of God. This is the pattern throughout *Psalm 107.*

I want to take some of the principles found in this Psalm and create an acrostic for the word THRIVE. Let this be a challenge for your family. When you are tempted to go your own way, look at what God really desires for you and your family. Trust Him to show you the path He has planned for you. Believe that He has a purpose for your blending family. And resolve to THRIVE.

Thanksgiving. I counted five different occurrences of the Psalmist admonition to "give thanks to the Lord." Are you thankful? Do you look for ways to express your thanks to God for your family and what He is doing? Approach your blending family with a heart of thanksgiving. *"Give thanks for the Lord, for He is good; His love endures forever." Psalm 107:1*

Healing. Do you recognize the healing God has brought in your life and in your family? Each of you have experienced pain to get to where you are today. Regardless of the reason for your previous family's end, God has a plan. You have a family that "died." But God did not leave you in the grave. He has sent His Word to heal you. He has rescued your family from the grave, and given you a new life in a new family. The Psalmist says, *"He sent forth his word and healed them; he rescued them from the grave." Psalm 107:20*

Redemption. As you come together as a family, trust God to redeem every single member of your family. Trust God for eternal redemption, but also trust Him to redeem the past. Mistakes, loss, hurt, failure, pain, brokenness ... all the things that brought you together as a family. Give them to God. Allow His redemption to renew your family. *"Let the redeemed of the Lord say this – those He redeemed from the hand of the foe, those He gathered from the lands, from east and west, from north and south." Psalm 107:2.*

Implore. God longs to bring you back to Himself. His desire is to restore you and your family. Are you willing to cry out to Him? Are you willing to trust Him to bring you back to Himself? Be willing to implore God with the future of your family. Even in the midst of their sin, those in this Psalm would cry out to God for help. In every case, not only did God hear their cries, but He saved and delivered them. *"Then they cried to the Lord in their trouble, and He saved them from their distress." Psalm 107:19*

Vibrant. God doesn't just half-way fill the need you have. He is generous and abundant in His answers. Look at the hope you have in Him. In this Psalm alone we see that He led the distressed and homeless to places where they could settle and be satisfied. He delivered the prisoner from the darkness and broke the chains of bondage. He healed the fool and rescued him from the grave. He stilled the storm to a whisper and hushed the waves of the sea. He turned the deserts into pools of water and parched ground into flowing springs. He brought prosperity where there had been poverty. He doesn't want to just help you and your family get by. He wants you to THRIVE!

Endurance. This entire Psalm is all about hope. God gives you the ability to endure, no matter the circumstance. You may feel as though your blending family will never be peaceful. You may doubt that your home could ever be a place of rest and joy. But God is a God of enduring hope. Chaos and confusion is not something God desires. He wants to provide peace and rest. He longs to give us a refuge. *"They were glad when it grew calm, and he guided them to their desired haven." Psalm 107:30.*

Endurance is good reminder that you are in your [re]marriage for the duration. The divorce rate for subsequent marriages is higher than for first time marriages. In our culture, endurance is sometimes foreign to blending families. However, God provides an opportunity to break this cycle.

🐾 How can you apply the THRIVE principle to your blending family? Take each letter of the acrostic and consider a personal example from your family.

Thanksgiving. Record the things you are thankful for in your blending family. Refer to this list when you are discouraged. Express thanks to God for these things in prayer.

Healing. Where is your family in the healing cycle? What are some things you can do to help the process? Record your thoughts. Pray especially for anyone in your family who is struggling to experience healing.

Redemption. Thank God for the redemption you are experiencing as your blending family grows. Are there things God is bringing to mind He desires to redeem in your family? Record your thoughts.

Implore. When trouble comes, remember to call upon God. Ask God to bring to mind the times when you have gone to Him for help and He has answered. If you are currently experiencing "trouble," give it God. You may want to write out a prayer.

Vibrant. Spend some time reflecting on the times in your blending family when God generously cared for a need. Record your memory. If you have a current need, pray for it and thank God that He is generous in His answers.

Endurance. God longs for you to endure in your blending family. What are some areas where your endurance is being challenged? Write them down. Then next to each one, write the word HOPE. Remember, there is always hope when you allow God to take over. *"Now may the God of hope fill you with all joy and peace in believing, that you may abound in hope by the power of the Holy Spirit." Romans 15:13 (NASB).* Spend some time meditating on this verse.

Read Psalm 107 again.

Ask God to speak clearly to you. Ask Him to show you where you are in the cycle you see in this Psalm. Are you in rebellion? Are you refusing to follow Him and His ways? Perhaps you are at the point where you are exhausted and without answers. You just can't do it anymore. Maybe you are crying out to God to deliver you and bring you out. Perhaps you are looking back at all God has done for you and it's time for you to just rejoice and thank

Him for His faithfulness. Allow Him to speak to you and encourage you wherever you are. Recognize the beautiful picture this Psalm paints. Man falls away every time. He rebels and walks in his own way. But God is faithful. Each time man cries out, God hears and answers. Cry out. He will hear you. He will answer you.

So what are "all these things" that God will add to those who seek Him first? God has everything you need to be a successful, joyful, peaceful family. As you seek Him first, He is faithful to meet the needs of you and your family. Whatever is lacking, He will provide. He is the source of everything you need to live victoriously. He is faithful to equip, encourage and empower you and your family to THRIVE.

Week Five

Who Cares!

"Blessed are the merciful, for they shall be shown mercy." Matthew 5:7

The first week of our study gave us the opportunity to look at the beatitudes in another translation. As I considered this week's study, I was reminded of the way The Message put this one. *"You're blessed when you care. At the moment of being 'care-full,' you find yourselves cared for."*

Sometimes I think we forget how powerful the simple action of caring for another really is. As a blending family, we often live with hurting people. We live with children who miss a parent who is either absent, or no longer involved in their life in the way they once were. We are in a marriage that began as a result of brokenness. Your spouse may or may not have found healing before joining with you. You may even have some unresolved struggles as you try to find your place and your way in a new family and marriage.

It's easy to feel bogged down, with little light at the end of the tunnel. In fact, you may not even be able to see the end of the tunnel. But I love the new perspective this beatitude invites. Jesus asks us to care for others.

Sometimes, in a blending family, we forget the importance of caring for others. We get so wrapped up in our own pain and perhaps healing, that we forget there are others on the journey with us. Early in our marriage, we were sometimes challenged with caring. While the desire to care was great, the ability to care was sometimes difficult. We can so easily be buried in our own hurt that we are unable to really reach out to another and help them carry their hurt. Especially when there are children who really need our support and encouragement on their journey.

Although we may feel buried in our own struggles, an amazing thing happens when we reach out and care for another. In our caring, we experience healing ourselves. I think that's exactly the principle Jesus was teaching in this verse. It is in giving care that we are able to best receive care and healing.

Are you ready to be care-full? Perhaps Jesus is challenging you in the way of care. A tough concept, maybe. But this week we will peel back the layers and look at what genuine Godly care looks like in the lives of others. Especially those with whom we share the most intimate of relationships.

Day One

Mercy and Grace

Before we can really begin to apply the concept of being merciful, we must first understand what Jesus means by merciful. While we've briefly discussed mercy as it relates to having a caring heart, there is more to the idea. When Jesus spoke to His disciples, He exhorted them to show mercy. It is important to understand what Jesus meant by this. What exactly is mercy?

Often times I think we hear the terms grace and mercy used interchangeably. But, while they sound like the same thing, there is an important distinction between the two. I recently heard an interview with Henry Blackaby, the author of *Experiencing God*. I like what he had to say about mercy. Here is the distinction he made. He explained that *grace* is God giving us something we don't deserve. No one can earn grace, or even be good enough to receive it on merit. Grace is a free gift. Something we receive that we don't deserve.

Mercy, on the other hand, prevents us getting what we actually do deserve. While God's judgment is what we deserve, God's mercy protects us from that judgment. God's mercy protects us from what we deserve in order that we are in a position to receive His grace, which we don't deserve. Ponder for a moment the power in the distinction between the two.

So, what is Jesus teaching in this beatitude? He says that we should refrain from giving people what they deserve, letting go of our perceived rights over others. It is akin to loving our neighbor as ourselves. We have the chance to consider the needs of others. In our family, we can set aside our own perceived rights in order to serve or care for others. Imagine what life with your family would be like if everyone considered others over themselves? Sounds like a bit of heaven on earth, doesn't it?

Practically speaking, it is having the attitude of Christ. This attitude requires that we treat others better than they deserve to be treated. When you encounter a situation where you feel wronged, how do you choose to respond? Do you insist on feeling justified, or are you willing to give the benefit of the doubt to the other person? Are you willing to serve another when they never reciprocate? Can you let go of your need for revenge when another has wronged you?

Jesus' encouragement is to let go of your need to seek justice in the face of personal injustice. He actually shows us the other side of the coin. Just as we have felt mistreated by another, perhaps we have been the one to mistreat. If you want to be shown mercy by another, Jesus says, show mercy. That means being willing to **not** give someone what they deserve.

When dealing with an ex-spouse there is always an opportunity to rehearse the wrongs committed against you. But Jesus would say to have an attitude of mercy. Let them off the hook. Allow God to deal with them. And allow God to deal with your own heart. Release your need for revenge into God's Hands. Let Him work in your heart. Choose to be merciful. Let's look at what else Jesus had to say about mercy.

Read Matthew 12:1-8.

What did the Pharisees accuse Jesus and His disciples of doing?

What do you think Jesus was trying to say to them with His response?

What does Jesus tell them in *Matthew 12:7*?

In this passage, Jesus and His disciples are hungry on the Sabbath. As they pass through a grain field, they pick some of the heads of grain in order to satisfy their hunger. When the Pharisees saw this, they condemned Jesus and His disciples for breaking the law. You may remember that the Pharisees, in their zeal to use good works to show their religiosity, had come up with hundreds of laws, rules and regulations for the Israelites to follow. The legalism had become burdensome and motivated by actions rather than the heart.

But remember what God said in *Deuteronomy 6:4*? His desire was that those who chose to follow Him would love Him with all their heart, soul and strength. He longed for their obedience to Him to be motivated by a heart of love for Him rather than simply an obligation to follow the law. Jesus wanted the Pharisees to see they were missing the point. Following God is as much about your heart as it is about your feet. It's one thing to obey out of resentful obligation. It is another thing altogether to obey out of a heart of love and devotion.

Think of your spouse. Let's say they have done something to upset you. In an attempt to make amends, they bring you flowers and your favorite drink from the local coffee shop. While it is a nice gesture, let's assume they really aren't that interested in how you feel. They just want out of the dog house. When you know their heart really isn't in the reconciliation, how much do those gifts, though very sweet, really mean to you? Aren't you looking more for a heart that is genuinely sorry that they've upset you? Wouldn't you rather have a sincere conversation about what happened than just receive empty gifts?

This is what Jesus is saying about our sacrifice. You see, God is much more interested in the heart of the one who brings the sacrifice, than He is in the sacrifice itself. God desires to have our heart, love and devotion. He doesn't want empty sacrifices. So the lesson is, if you're going to bring home a guilt offering, make sure the flowers and coffee come with a sincere heart.

In this passage, Jesus is trying to tell the Pharisees they are missing the point completely. They are face-to-face with the long-awaited Messiah, yet they can't see **Him** because they are blinded by their own empty legalism.

So what does this have to do with your being merciful in your family? God longs for you to share **His** heart of compassion with your family. While it will likely not be easy, God is much more interested in your heart when you show compassion than the acts of compassion you might be compelled to share.

Perhaps there is some "heart work" God may want to do today. The lesson is short, yet the concept requires much consideration. Spend some time in prayer asking God to speak to your heart about grace and mercy. Allow Him to show you areas where you can show mercy to someone in your family. Pray for the person in your family who is the most difficult for you to show mercy.

Has God spoken to you today regarding grace and mercy? Record what you heard.

What are some areas of your life where God wants you to show mercy to someone in your family?

Who is the one person in your blending family most difficult for you and why?

How do you believe God wants you to relate and respond to that person?

From your perspective, what is the difference between grace and mercy?

Which is most difficult for you and why?

Today's lesson isn't easy. But God wants to do a work in you and your family. Resolve today to be the one who will be the example of caring in your family. Show mercy. Care for others. Then, watch and see what God will do.

Day Two

Forgiveness

Yesterday we looked at what God's word had to say about grace and mercy. Do you remember the difference?

Record what you remember about grace.

Record what you remember about mercy.

The lessons this week may be difficult. We will deal with subjects that everyone struggles with. We in blending families often have more opportunities to practice these spiritual disciplines because of our circumstances.

I recently heard a sermon on today's topic. I was encouraged because the sermon was for everyone; not just blending families. That tells me that today's study is the great normalizer across all circumstances.

Before we jump into our study, spend some time in prayer. You will likely be challenged today. Ask God to prepare your heart to hear from Him and be willing to follow what He reveals. As He does a work in your heart, I think you will be amazed at the freedom that comes as you resolve to walk in obedience.

Forgiveness. We desire to receive it. However, it may one of the hardest things to give. We will look at what God's Word has to say about forgiveness, but will also make some practical application. I want you to have more than just a knowledge about forgiveness. I want you to be able to experience it in your life and relationships.

Before we step into the scripture, let's look at the definition of forgiveness. A practical, understandable definition says that forgiveness is releasing or letting go of your right to hurt someone else for hurting you. You may have been betrayed by your ex-spouse. You may have been unfairly accused by someone at work. Your children may have resentment toward you because of untruths they've been told by another family member. There may have been a loss from the negligence of another. You may have been the victim of a horrific crime committed by someone you don't even know. You may have been abused at the hand of a family member who was supposed to love and protect you. There are many things which happen to us throughout our life that provide opportunities for us to forgive.

As we begin to look into the spiritual discipline of forgiveness, there are a few things that are important to understand. A recent study by Christian statistician George Barna reveals the following misconceptions about forgiveness. It is important to understand what forgiveness is **not** before we can embrace what forgiveness really is. Let's cover these first.

Forgiveness must be earned. Not. This myth says I cannot let go of my own bitterness until someone else earns it. The truth is that I have no control over the actions or attitudes of another. Do I allow my perceptions about the one who I am called to forgive control whether I actually forgive them? Can the feelings of unforgiveness I harbor bring any kind of restitution? The most damaging part of this misconception is that I cannot move forward with my own life until I receive whatever restitution I think is necessary. When you are waiting on another to earn your forgiveness, you have given them power over you and your feelings. Until **you** release them, you have strapped them on your back and are carrying them around with you. You can never be free of them until you release them. Doing so means you are no longer bound to the offender. You become free to live your life without carrying the oppressive anxieties from the one who has hurt you.

Forgiveness is a once-for-all decision. Not. This myth states, once I choose to forgive the one who offended me, I will never again have to deal with it. The problem is, in our human nature we are unable to release our hurt once and for all. Forgiveness often requires that we forgive over and over again for the same offense. Many disciplines of our faith are a process rather than an event. God is the One who is doing a work in us when we allow God to forgive through us. Trust the process. Each time your heart struggles to forgive, go back to God and ask Him for the grace to forgive. Again and again.

Forgiveness means forgetting. Not. All my life I've been taught that God forgives and then He forgets my transgression. I even have substantial scripture references upon which to stand. However, I recently heard a sermon clarifying God's treatment of forgiveness. *Psalm 103:12* reminds us that *"as far as the east is from the west, so far are our transgressions from us when forgiven by God."* *Jeremiah 31:34* tells us that God will forgive our iniquity and our sin He will remember no more.

What scripture actually teaches through these references is not that God erases the transgression, but that because of His love for me, and the sacrifice of Christ on the cross, He no longer holds me accountable for the debt my transgressions have accrued. These are not literal descriptions of God erasing a memory from His mind, but a spiritual principle that teaches that He sees the transgression as paid in full. He doesn't see my transgression without seeing the stamp that says paid-in-full.

In our human nature, we are incapable of forgetting what has been done to us. Our mind does not have the biological capabilities to erase itself. Therefore, forgiveness is a spiritual choice. While we will carry the memory of the offense throughout our life, we no longer have to carry the burden of the offense. Spiritually, we can release the offender.

Forgiveness equals reconciliation. Not. Some of us may have chosen the path of unforgiveness because we see a reconciled relationship as impossible. Forgiveness does not automatically presuppose the relationship will be restored. Consider the players. If someone has wronged you, you have the choice to forgive. You can forgive whether or not they ask or whether or not they ever do anything to make amends or offer restitution for the offense. You are the only player in the action of forgiveness. Reconciliation, on the other hand, requires that both players come together and have a mutual interaction that will restore or mend the relationship. Adultery has ended a marriage. While you are perfectly free to forgive the adulterous spouse, reconciliation did not happen. You or your ex-spouse, or both, chose to move on. Reconciliation is not a choice you made. Perhaps you were robbed by a business associate. Would it be prudent to enter into another business relationship where you would be financially vulnerable, or would the wisdom of separating professionally prevail? Forgiveness and reconciliation are two separate transactions. Sometimes you will experience both. Sometimes you will only experience forgiveness.

Forgiveness is a one-way street while reconciliation is a two-way street. Even though reconciliation can be a result of forgiveness, it is not the indicator that forgiveness has occurred or been completed.

Consider any of these fallacies that you may have embraced. Are there things you need to reconsider in light of what you've learned? Are there any of these that have stopped your ability to forgive? Pause and pray about these things before we continue our study. Now, let's step into God's Word to see what He has to teach about what forgiveness **is**.

🐾 *Read Matthew 18:21-35.*

While this is probably a very familiar passage, I want us to look at what God is really teaching. Jesus loved to use parables to teach deep spiritual truths. He had a remarkable way of telling a story so that the point or moral of the story could change a life. This particular parable is prompted by a question from Peter. He comes to Jesus with a question about forgiveness. The question seems to come on the heels of a teaching that could possibly have given the "spiritual folks" an opportunity to become a little pious. They had just discussed how to correct a brother who was found to be in sin. I think we can all feel a little bit proud when reading *Matthew 18:15-20*, because we consider ourselves to be the one who is tasked with bringing correction to a brother. I think Jesus is quick to turn the tables.

The plot is very understandable. It involved a man who owed a large debt. The lowly, indebted servant is summoned to the king who wants to settle all the debts owed him. This servant, in a panic realizes that he owes a debt he could never repay. I did some research into exactly what the worth of ten thousand talents would equal in today's money. The closest equivalent in today's US dollars would put the debt somewhere around $16 billion dollars. Obviously, this was a debt that could never be repaid by the low-income servant. The servant owed a debt that could not even be paid by a wealthy man. It was more money than he could ever earn or repay. The enormity of the debt was impossible to settle. Yet, in his mercy, the king forgave all of the servant's debt.

As you might expect, he left the king's presence a new man. A man relieved of an impossible debt. This man would have lost his family and spent the remainder of his days in a debtor's prison. Yet the compassion of the king allowed him to have his life back. His wife and children were saved. He was free to continue his life without the burden of the debt. Imagine being in a situation where your home was going into foreclosure. Instead of getting a call from the bank telling you to be out by the end of the week, they instead inform you they have decided to "write off" or completely forgive the debt you owe and cannot pay. You went from the fear of being homeless to having a home free and clear of debt.

After receiving such an incredible gift, you would think the man would be so grateful that he would pour out his own gratitude and generosity over everyone he encountered. Yet the story Jesus told takes a different turn.

There was a fellow servant who owed this guy a hundred denarii. So, the first thing the grateful servant did was to go and forgive the debt his fellow servant owed him, right? Just a hundred denarii. In today's currency that equaled about $16. You read that correctly. Just $16. Not impossible to pay back, but the servant's friend needed a little bit of time to come up with the money. The debt really was not even enough to worry about. Surely, that small debt would be forgiven considering the enormity of the debt-forgiveness the first man received. Yet this is not how the story unfolds. Instead of forgiving his fellow servant, the unmerciful servant (as my Bible titles this section) goes to his friend and demands repayment. The owing servant fell to his knees and begged his friend for time. Over time, it would be possible to repay the debt. But instead of even allowing the fellow servant an extension on the debt, he immediately had the man thrown into prison.

Great story, right? How could that servant who had been forgiven so much, be so unforgiving of so little? And that was Jesus' point. Let me just spell it out.

We are the servant who owes a debt that can never be repaid. My sin has accumulated a debt I could never repay no matter how hard I labor or what I sacrificed. I could never repay the debt. What I deserve is to lose everything I have and everyone I love and be thrown into prison for all eternity. Yet, God in His mercy looks upon me with compassion and chooses to forgive the entire debt. It is a gift to me. The unmerciful servant in the story didn't have to do anything for the king. He just had to receive and reciprocate the gift of forgiveness.

I think the question Jesus would want us to ponder in this story, is, as the one who has been forgiven a debt we could never repay, how freely do we forgive others? My sin put God's Son on the cross. And although what I have experienced at the hand of another may have been horrific, if God can forgive me and release me from the debt I owe Him, what stops me from offering the same compassion to the one who has sinned against me?

Today has likely been a difficult lesson. Forgiveness seems to be one of the most difficult spiritual disciplines we encounter. We will resume our study of forgiveness tomorrow, but for today, you have an assignment.

Think about the person who is the most difficult for you to forgive. It may be a parent. It may be a boss. It may be your ex-spouse. It may be your new mate. It may be a friend who has betrayed you. Write their name or initials here:

Think about what they did that you need to forgive. You can write it down here, if you would like to.

Think about why it is so difficult for you to forgive them. Is there a feeling you are hanging onto? Does it seem as though they have come off scot-free when they are the one who has done all the damage? Does it feel like they haven't had to pay for what they have done to you? Record your thoughts and feelings below. Be as specific as you need to be.

Now, spend some time with God. Tell Him what they did to you. Tell Him how you feel. Don't try to "spiritualize" what you are feeling. Just tell Him honestly how you feel. Finally, one-by-one give Him the feelings and thoughts you are holding onto about the one for whom you need to offer forgiveness. Thank Him for giving you the courage and strength to begin the process of forgiveness.

Day Three

Still Forgiving

I hope your experience yesterday was a beginning as you seek to forgive. Perhaps it was a chance for you to continue in a process of forgiveness that had stalled. Maybe it was just a time of celebration and confirmation that God has done an amazing work in your heart with regard to forgiveness. As we work on day two of forgiveness, my prayer is that you will continue to grow in your ability to forgive. The power and freedom we experience can perform miracles as we allow forgiveness to become a way of life. I want us to revisit what we began in yesterday's study. If you need to refresh your memory, reread the story in *Matthew 18:21-35*.

Today, I want us to consider the practical application of the principles Jesus taught in this passage. Remember, our focus for the week is mercy. Extending mercy means you are withholding what someone deserves. For our purposes, you are no longer holding on to your need for your offender to pay for the hurt or pain they have caused you. Here are some practical helps that may encourage you as you seek to live a life of forgiveness.

Forgiveness is a choice, not a feeling. The king in our parable had to make a choice. While Jesus' story doesn't let us in on the thoughts or feelings of the king, I would imagine he had to do some internal volleying before coming to the decision to forgive. You are no different than the king. When someone who owes a debt to you stands before you, you have a choice. Although your feelings might not agree, you can make a conscious choice to forgive. *"Therefore, since Christ suffered in his body, arm yourselves also with the same attitude, because He who has suffered in His body is done with sin. As a result, He does not live the rest of His earthly life for evil human desires, but rather for the will of God" 1 Peter 4:1-2.*

👣 Have you chosen to forgive? If not, what is standing in your way?

Forgiveness won't be easy. When the king decided to forgive the servant of his debt, the king knew that it would be personally costly. The servant owed him. The servant had done nothing to make amends or to repay the debt he had incurred at the expense of the king. When you are faced with the choice to forgive, it may be a tough choice to make because there may never be, in your eyes, appropriate restitution or repayment for what has been taken from you. *"Be kind and compassionate to one another, forgiving each other, just as in Christ God forgave you" Ephesians 4:32.*

❧ What is the major obstacle in the way of your forgiving someone who has offended you?

Ask God to take the obstacle away so that you can choose to forgive.

The power to forgive is not in the strength of the flesh, but the strength of the Spirit. I'm not sure that any human being has the natural capacity to forgive. I think, deep down inside, we are just very tall two-year-olds. If we let our flesh loose, we want things our own way. We want what we want, when we want it and how we want it. Life is all about us. When someone does us wrong, they should pay ... and pay dearly. But fortunately, we don't have to rely on ourselves to offer forgiveness. After all, God is the master of forgiveness. He forgives each one of us for every single sin. He understands forgiveness in a way we can't. And He has the power to forgive in way we don't. Trust God's power, presence, strength and work in you to be the catalyst as you forgive. *"I can do all things through Christ who strengthens me" Philippians 4:13.*

❧ If you allow the Spirit to empower you to forgive, what are the benefits?

Spend some time in prayer asking God to help you forgive.

Forgiving means letting go. I have a mental picture that helps me when I struggle to forgive. I imagine the person who I have not been able to forgive being strapped onto my back. They are tied tightly to me. I'm the one doing all the work. I have to carry them around. They know everything I do. They go everywhere I go. They hear every conversation and are an intimate part of my life. I am allowing them to weigh me down and keep me from doing what I really want to do. They stop me from going where I want to go. And honestly, I am exhausted from the constant weight of them on my back. If I really want to experience a relief from the burden in order to have true freedom, I need to cut the rope and let them go. They no longer have a right into my life or the power to weigh me down or stop me from doing what I want to do or going where I want to go. *"But thanks be to God that, though you used to be slaves to sin, you wholeheartedly obeyed the form of teaching to which you were entrusted" Romans 6:17.* Choose to forgive wholeheartedly.

✒ Consider what your life would be like if you could truly let go of the offense and offender. Record your thoughts.

Forgiveness is freedom. Perhaps a practical example would have to do with an ex-relationship. Maybe it's an ex-spouse or ex-in-law. Maybe it's a parent. Maybe it's an ex-friend or an ex-business associate. You have been wronged. You have been hurt. You have lost something vital in your life at the hands of another. But when you choose to forgive and release your right to cause them harm, you are truly free. After all, can restitution really occur? Your ex-spouse has torn apart your family. Can they really repay all the hurt and pain they have caused as a result? That ex-business associate who has robbed you financially; can they really repay all they have taken? Sure they may can return the dollars, but can they restore the trust that was broken? What about a parent who abused you or allowed another to abuse you. By holding on to the unforgiveness, can you really get back what was taken from you? If you really want freedom, you must choose to forgive. The unmerciful servant's unwillingness to forgive the debt owed him cost him his freedom. He was forever confined and tortured. Don't allow your unforgiveness to confine and torture you. *"It is for freedom that Christ has set us free. Stand firm, then, and do not let yourselves be burdened again by a yoke of slavery" Galatians 5:1.*

✒ What is the bondage holding you hostage? What do you need to do to become truly free?

Keep forgiveness in context. When you are tempted to hold a grudge, remember how much God has forgiven you. In the parable, the ten thousand talents were forgiven. A debt that could never be repaid was counted as paid in full. It was the hundred denarii that caused the issue. Such a small, insignificant debt. It seems unfathomable that the servant forgiven for so much could be so petty in refusing to forgive so little. *"But God demonstrates his own love for us in this: While we were **still sinners**, Christ died for us" Romans 5:8 (emphasis mine).* God didn't wait on me to make a change in my life before He forgave me. Paul says that while I was still a slave to sin, Christ died for me. The forgiveness of Christ was available to me while I was unworthy. And I am still unworthy, yet God chooses to forgive me. How could I *not* forgive the debt of another against me?

🐚 Allow God to speak to your heart. Ask Him to remind you of times when you have been forgiven. Thank Him for His forgiveness. Consider how you have been forgiven when you find it difficult to forgive another.

Forgiveness is God's will. All throughout scripture, God's people are challenged to live counter-culturally. While the world says take all you can and can all you get, God says be generous and give away what you have. Society says to take, while God says to give. The world says get even, and God says forgive. The world says to hate your enemy but God says to love them. The world says pursue happiness but God challenges us to pursue holiness.

As difficult as it may be to understand, God wills that we forgive others. And He doesn't make exceptions. God doesn't say to forgive others unless they …. And then provides a list of righteous excuses for us to refuse to offer forgiveness. Spend time in prayer. Ask God to reveal any area of rebellion you have about forgiveness. Who is the one person in your life who is most difficult to forgive? Allow God to speak to your heart and help you forgive.

Forgiveness heals our bitterness. One of the greatest examples of forgiveness in scripture is the story of Joseph. Because of his brothers' jealously, he was sold into slavery. Eventually he worked his way into Potiphar's household. Potiphar, an Egyptian official, had placed Joseph in charge of his entire household. After being falsely accused of raping Potiphar's wife, Joseph was incarcerated. After his release from prison, he was placed in charge of the entire land of Egypt. You can read about Joseph's life in *Genesis 37-50*. It is really a great story of a man who could have rightfully adopted a defeatist attitude that says "can't win for losing," yet he remained faithful to God. He was committed to live his life God's way.

If you read the story, you will see the way Joseph chose to respond to all the injustices in his life. He was left for dead by his brothers. He was sold into slavery as a result of their disdain for him. His father was told he was dead. He was falsely accused by Potiphar's wife. He was put in prison. Yet in all these cases, Joseph forgave his offenders.

After he had been put in charge of Egypt, God warned him that a famine was coming. He was to put back provision from the seven years of prosperity in order to save the people in the famine. In a bitter twist of irony, Joseph's brothers came to him for help. However, they did not recognize Joseph as the brother they had betrayed all those years ago. Yet Joseph recognized them. And instead of seeking revenge, he showed compassion. How was Joseph able to respond with such forgiveness?

🐚 *Read Genesis 50:15-21.*

Joseph chose to see his own life through the eyes of God. Hurt is a bitter truth to life. Some of our deepest hurts are inflicted at the hands of those closest to us. Although we can't change what has been done to us, like Joseph, we can choose our perspective. Joseph was able to see beyond the hurt and pain of the rejection of his brothers, and see God's hand of redemption. God was able to use what was intended for harm, to bring about good. Joseph saw God intervene to take the pain and hurt and use it to save thousands of lives.

We see a restatement of the same concept by Paul in his letter to the Romans. *Romans 8:28* says *"And we know that in all things God works for the good of those who love him, who have been called according to his purpose."* You can trust God with the things that have happened to you and the ways you may have been wronged by others. Just like Joseph, God has a plan to redeem the painful experiences you have had at the hands of others.

&. Consider a time when you have been hurt at the hands of someone close to you. How did you choose to respond?

If you held onto unforgiveness, how has that affected you?

If you were able to forgive that person, how has your life been impacted?

If you are holding on to unforgiveness, think about how your life would be different if you chose to release it and forgive. Record your thoughts.

Forgiveness gives us a future of hope. There are a number of scriptures that come to mind when considering how the past impacts us. We can allow the past to completely cripple us and prevent us from experiencing all God desires for our present and future. But one of my favorite passages puts it like this: *"Not that I have already obtained all this, or have already been made perfect, but I press on the take hold of that for which Christ Jesus took hold of me. Brothers, I do not consider myself yet to have taken hold of it. But one thing I do: Forgetting what is behind and straining toward what is ahead, I press on toward the goal to win the prize for which God has called me heavenward in Christ Jesus"* Philippians 3:12-14.

We can't change the past. We can't undo mistakes we've made or regrets we may have. But we can stop the past from crippling our present. It really all boils down to choices.

You can begin today to change how you respond. You can begin today to let go of past hurt and pain and choose to forgive. When Paul talks about "forgetting what is behind," I don't think he actually means that we are able to not remember. You are not forcing your mind to pretend it didn't happen, but you are letting go of the power the past has over your present. Paul is speaking to our focus. Instead of erasing a memory, we are re-framing our perspective of the past. God wants us to look ahead. Paul says he will press on toward the goal, toward the prize that awaits him. The challenge to each of us is no different. Are you willing to let go of the power of the past, and begin to look toward the future?

What choices can you make today that will propel you toward the future God has planned for you?

Today is the past of tomorrow. While today is still the present, make decisions and choices that will prevent tomorrow's past from being filled with regret. You can't change the past that is already written, but today is a new page. A new story. Resolve that what you do today will be tomorrow's memory of victory.

I know the study today may have reopened some old wounds. Maybe it has shed some light on some long-buried unforgiveness. If so, let today be a new beginning on your journey to experience true freedom in forgiveness. I also want to challenge you to do some soul-searching with regard to your current family.

Are you harboring any unforgiveness for anyone?

Is there a child in your home that has offended you (or perhaps continues to offend you) and you have held a grudge?

Has your spouse done or said something that has hurt you and for whatever reason you are finding it difficult to forgive?

Let today be a fresh start. Choose to forgive. Choose to live a life-style of forgiveness. Tear up the record of wrongs you have been using to keep score. Release your need for revenge. Let go of your list of demands. Trust God to help you wake up every morning with a new resolve that for this day, you will be a fountain of forgiveness.

What you have certainly discovered is that if you allow yourself to love, you are opening yourself up to pain. Your spouse will say and do things to hurt your feelings. Your children will say mean things to you and disappoint you. But what will you choose to do with those things?

Day Four

Trust

As we begin today's study, we will look at how trust plays a vital role in our ability to forgive over time. While this is a Bible study and not a paper on psychology, there are certain principles from the study of psychology that apply.

We learned earlier this week that forgiveness is often a choice before it is a feeling. We also saw that forgiveness is not a once-for-all decision. While our salvation is a once-for-all decision and cannot be rescinded, forgiveness is often an ongoing choice. Each encounter we have with our ex-spouse may be an opportunity to choose forgiveness.

The passage we studied this week began with a simple question pondering how many times one must forgive. While the legalists would take Jesus' response and make a math equation out of it (not just seven, but seventy times seven), I think Jesus' point was that we forgive however many times forgiveness is required. That means sometimes we will be tempted to take the offense back and rescind the forgiveness. Other times there may be a recurring offense that will be forgiven over and over.

I have to take a moment here to clarify. If the recurring offense is abuse or infidelity, that requires a different response. Yes, forgive. As many times as you are offended, forgive. However, in these cases, you are not obligated to stay in the relationship. If you or your children are in danger or if your spouse is habitually unfaithful or unwilling to give up the adulterous relationship, you have the right and responsibility to seek safety and have a biblical foundation upon which to leave or ask the offending party to leave. Although there are no implicit biblical instructions for someone suffering from abuse, the Bible is certainly replete with admonitions about the treatment of others. If you are in danger, get out. If your mate is unfaithful and unrepentant, you have biblical grounds to dissolve the relationship.

However, an additional point of clarification is called for as well. Some marriages survive infidelity. Just because a spouse has been adulterous doesn't mean you are commanded to leave. I know a number of couples who have survived and even grown through an affair. Although not the subject of our study today, these are things that require additional help. You and your mate certainly need to seek counsel from a professional counselor or trusted pastor.

With that said, we can begin to look at how we can forge a strong relationship built on forgiveness. In the world of psychology, forgiveness and trust are often linked. Regardless of the offense we are called upon to forgive, there is often a loss of trust that must be rebuilt. If your spouse does something that is hurtful to you, you lose trust in them with regard to that one thing. For example, you may have asked your spouse to do something. It might be a leaky faucet that needs to be fixed. It might be calling you to let you know they are on their way home. It might be requesting 15 minutes of solitude as soon as they get home. For whatever reason, these requests are not met and the result is hurt. Of course, your offending spouse isn't intentionally hurtful. These are just things that are a struggle to remember or difficult to do.

Over time, how these scenarios play out can impact your marriage. While it may not seem like a big thing, there are likely underlying reasons that this is something important. You may be completely innocent in just being so overwhelmed every day that you forget what has been requested. But regardless of the "why's," without forgiveness, this could become a major obstacle in your marriage. A small infraction, over time, can grow into an enormous issue.

This begins to whittle away at trust. You begin to build walls of distrust when you have needs or requests that go unmet and unanswered. Eventually, these minor struggles can grow into major issues. But in order to begin to rebuild trust, forgiveness must first take place.

Now, let's see what God's Word has to teach us about trust. Forgiveness and trust are definitely related. It is difficult to develop a trusting relationship where unforgiveness remains. Unforgiveness is the greatest barrier to trust. Once someone has broken trust, forgiveness is the essential first step in rebuilding trust. Forgiveness is the key that opens the door to trust.

There is a trust theory studied in Psychology. Some psychologists have adopted an acronym describing the process of rebuilding trust. Trust is not something that is instantly obtained. It is something that is developed over time. Once trust is broken, it takes time and intentionality to rebuild. In order to understand this, I want to share this textbook principle because, to me, it accurately describes the process. The letters SAD relate to the actions of the one who has broken trust.

Sincerity. Once trust has been broken, the offending party has the opportunity to begin to rebuild trust. Do you believe that your offender is sincere in their remorse and willingness to change? This is the first step to rebuilding trust.

Ability. Is your offender able to make amends? Are they able to make a change in order to rebuild trust? When trust has been broken, there is the need to see a change in the behavior that has been forgiven. Forgiving does not mean accepting the offense over and over. Remember, forgiveness is letting go and releasing your right to hurt another for causing you pain. It is not ignoring the hurt. When you want to rebuild trust, you need to believe that your offender is truly able to change the offending behavior.

Duration. Trust is rebuilt over time. You see the sincerity of the desire to rebuild trust when the offender is making a change in their behavior. You see the change happen once or twice and you still are not very trusting. This could just be an accident, or because of their recent resolve, they are more aware of their behavior. But what happens over time will determine if trust is to truly be restored. Each time the offender takes a step that reinforces their sincerity and ability to make a change, another brick of trust is mortared into the wall.

Scripture provides a great example of trust being rebuilt. We are going to visit the life of the apostle Peter.

🐾 *Read Matthew 26:69-75.*

What did Peter do?

How many times did he do this?

When he realized what he had done, what was his response?

This is the story of Peter's denial of Christ. Just when Jesus needed His friends the most, they all left Him. And Peter, in all his passion, was perhaps the one who was the most vehement in his denial. When Jesus was trying to explain what was to come, and that his followers would all fall away, Peter was bold in his support of Jesus. Yet, when confronted after Jesus' arrest, Peter called down curses upon himself and denied with great fervor that he knew Christ.

For Jesus, Peter's denial probably brought incredible pain. Peter was one of the disciples closest to Jesus. He was one of the inner-circle. Peter had done the worst thing a friend could do. He had left Jesus and denied his friendship at the very time Jesus needed him the most. When is the last time you have felt betrayed by someone you love? Has someone in your family said or done something that has hurt you deeply? How have you responded to that hurt? Let's look at how Jesus ultimately rebuilt the relationship He had with Peter.

🐾 *Read John 21:15-17.*

What did Jesus ask Peter?

What did Jesus tell Peter to do?

How many times did Jesus ask the question of Peter?

While these passages may seem unrelated, they are a beautiful picture of Jesus' forgiveness and restored trust. When Jesus needed Peter at His side the most, Peter's fear caused him to deny that He even knew Jesus. In fact, Peter didn't just deny Christ once, but three times on the eve before Christ's crucifixion. When the resurrected Christ approached Peter, He asked an interesting question. He gave Peter the opportunity to affirm his love. And Jesus didn't just ask Peter once. He posed the question three times. Jesus gave Peter the opportunity to redeem all three denials. Each time, Jesus gave Peter a chance to build trust. While Jesus knew all along how Peter would respond, He allowed Peter to speak the words affirming his love for the Savior.

Building trust is a lifelong endeavor. Once broken, trust is rebuilt over time. Open your heart and allow God to help you trust again. If you are the offender, allow God to empower and equip you to earn back the trust you have lost.

Spend some time in prayer, asking God to help you on your journey of trust. Pray for the one who has lost your trust. Pray for the one whose trust you have lost. Pray that your family will become a safe place where trust is strong and faith in each other is powerful.

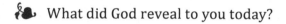 What did God reveal to you today?

Who are you having difficulty trusting and why?

What is your greatest doubt in trusting them? Do you doubt their sincerity? Is it their ability you struggle with? Are you waiting to see if the duration of the change will last?

What does God want you to do in releasing that doubt to Him?

Day Five

Prayer is the Key

Forgiveness and trust may very well be two of the most difficult disciplines God requires. Perhaps the foundational issue has to do with our focus on God over focus on self. Left to our own human nature, we will almost always respond in selfishness. But when God begins to do a transformation within our hearts, He has to tear down those walls of selfishness intrinsic in our nature. Not only does God desire that we look to Him first, but He also longs for us to experience the freedom we find in valuing others over ourselves. When I give my heart to God, I can begin to allow Him to do a new work within my heart that teaches me to consider the needs of others over my own selfishness.

This is not only a cultural paradigm shift, but requires that we live contrary to our own fleshly nature. What seems impossible, is possible when we learn to release all of our feelings to God. He has made a way for us to live in Godliness without having to depend on our weak self-will to succeed. So what is the key to living a life that exhibits mercy, grace, forgiveness and trust? In a word: prayer.

The disciples walked with Christ throughout His ministry. They observed Him perform miracles. They watched as He healed disease and freed captives from demons. They saw Him treat people with love. They watched Him deny Himself and treat others with dignity and compassion. They heard Him forgive people's sins. They watched His wisdom challenge the Jewish religious leaders. They also saw Him as He went to a place to be alone with His heavenly Father. The disciples apparently observed the power Jesus received through time spent with His Father. It is no surprise the one thing the disciples asked Jesus to teach them was how to pray. As we close this week's study, we are going to look at what Jesus taught His disciples regarding prayer. We are going to look at two parallel passages. Meaning, they record the same information, each providing a unique perspective.

&. *Read Luke 11:1-13.*

What was Jesus doing as the passage opens?

What did the disciples ask of Jesus?

Although scripture doesn't explicitly answer this question, take a minute and consider why you think the disciples would ask Jesus to teach them this one thing?

Jesus tells a story in *Luke 11:5-7.* What do you learn about prayer from the story?

Read *Luke 11:9.* What do you learn about prayer?

🔖 *Read Matthew 6:5-14.*

What is Matthew's warning about prayer?

How does Matthew instruct us to pray?

What is Matthew emphasizing when he warns about babbling?

In the next few verses, we find what most people refer to as the Lord's Prayer. Many of us have memorized the prayer, and we often recite it aloud. While Jesus offered this prayer as an illustration, it was never intended to be a mantra. Let's take a closer look at what Jesus suggested.

"Our Father in heaven." Our prayers are offered to the One True God. We pray not to gods, but to the God of Heaven. And while He is the creator God, Jesus uses an endearing term as He addresses God the Father. This not only points toward mankind's relationship with God as Creator, but also connotes our connection with the God who adopts all of us who accept Christ's gift of salvation. It is through that transaction we join the eternal family of God. Jesus is helping the disciples understand His purpose was to bring reconciliation between a Holy God and unholy man. Christ would bridge the gap and satisfy the sin-debt each of us owe. When we pray to God as our Father, we are acknowledging His Sovereignty as

Creator, but as those who have accepted Christ's gift of salvation we are also acknowledging Him as our personal Abba, Father.

The prayer can be broken down into six parts. The first three components refer to God's honor and the second three refer to our own needs. Let's look at each of these six petitions.

"Hallowed be your name." This statement is acknowledging God's honor and sovereignty. It means God's name is to be glorified or magnified. We bring honor to God simply for Who He is. As we approach a Holy God, we are taught to acknowledge exactly Who we are petitioning. This also speaks to our desire that in all our requests, God be honored and glorified.

"Your Kingdom come." Jesus is the Gospel message. He is the Gateway to the kingdom of God. Just as Christ preached the kingdom of God, so we are to pray that God's salvation through Christ would engulf the world. We are asking God to help us remain obedient to Him and His principles for living. We are praying that His people would *"walk in a manner worthy of Gospel of Christ."* God's literal Kingdom on earth is a future event. However, we can pray for God's purpose and plan to be at work on earth through the Holy Spirit-led lives of His followers.

"Your will be done on earth as it is heaven." God's will is the focus of this petition. God rules the heavens without rebellion. When we pray for God's will to be done on earth as it is in heaven, we are giving ourselves over to obedience. We are also praying that God would do such a work of redemption in the world that earth would be more like heaven.

"Give us this day our daily bread." Just like God provided for the delivered Israelites in the desert, so He will care for us today. He wants us to come to Him for our daily provision. The bread is for today, not tomorrow. In so doing, we remain dependent upon Him for our every need. It is important to realize Jesus was probably teaching that not only will God supply our physical need for sustenance, but He also longs to provide for our daily spiritual need as well. Scripture often uses bread to symbolize a spiritual filling as much as physical food. Jesus told His followers that He was the Bread of Life. Just before His crucifixion, He explained, like the bread, His body would be broken for them. Partaking of the bread is a picture of the acceptance of the sacrifice of His body as payment for sin. Jesus said that His "bread" was to do the will of His Father. So when we pray for our daily bread, we are asking God for more than just daily physical provision.

"Forgive us our debts as we have forgiven our debtors." We are acknowledging our need for forgiveness from sin. We are acknowledging that we have a sin-debt we cannot pay. We are trusting God to forgive the debt. We are also trusting Him for the strength and courage to forgive those who carry a sin-debt against us.

"And lead us not into temptation, but deliver us from the evil one." While God never uses evil to tempt us to stumble, He does allow the enemy to tempt us. While Satan would love nothing more than to watch us fail, God is all-powerful to help us overcome the temptation. The story of Job is a great example. God allowed Satan to touch Job's life in order that Job might be proven faithful. God never gave Satan free-reign over Job. God was always in control of what Satan could bring into Job's life. God wants us to be strengthened along this life's journey. Sometimes there are things in our lives that are difficult, but give us opportunity to trust God. While the enemy can and does try to draw us off the path, God is willing and able to deliver us from the evil one.

So, what does all this have to do with showing mercy in our household? Showing mercy by forgiving others is difficult. We don't have the willpower or strength to live a life of forgiveness. However, through the power of God, we can forgive because we have been forgiven. The best way to unleash that power is through prayer, acknowledging God for Who He is and what He can do in our heart and life.

In a blending family, you have limitless opportunities to forgive. You also have limitless opportunities to be forgiven. Trust God through prayer to make your family a family marked by forgiveness. Let God's Spirit so empower your family that your default becomes forgiveness.

What would your home be like if the default of your family was forgiveness? Spend some time journaling your thoughts.

As you end the study this week, use the Lord's Prayer as a model. Begin to pray for everyone in your household and ask God to give you the strength and courage to be a forgiver. Let your family experience the freedom found only in forgiveness.

Family Activity for Fun! Showing mercy to those in your home requires forgiveness. This week we've looked at the bondage we experience when we choose not to forgive. When I think of bondage, I think of being locked up in a prison. No freedom. Every single thing I do is controlled by someone else. I can only imagine how amazing it would feel to have my cell unlocked and to be told I am free. So, here's an idea for your family. Fill a basket with keys. Maybe you have old keys in drawers, or you might want to cut out paper keys. If time is short, just use strips of paper with the word "key" written on them. Get together with your family and explain that this week, you are going to try an experiment. Whenever someone does something to you requiring forgiveness, there is a choice to be made. If you choose to forgive them, take a key from the basket. Tell them they are forgiven. Give them a key. The key is a reminder you have forgiven them of their offense against you. Now, you take a key and keep it for yourself. This will serve as a reminder to you of your willingness to forgive. At the end of the week, come back together as a family and bring your keys. Talk about your experiences throughout the week. Close with a time of prayer as family, thanking God for helping you become a forgiving family.

Week Six

The Pure in Heart

"Blessed are the pure in heart, for they will see God." Matthew 5:8

He was a man of honor. A man called by God; set apart for God's purpose. He was a man after God's own heart. He was an unlikely leader, but one God had chosen and anointed to lead. He was faithful. God showed him favor in all his endeavors. By all accounts, this man was truly blessed.

Then there was that day. The man was in the stride of life. Successful and respected. Wealthy and held in high esteem. He had come into his own and was confident and contented with his life. He was so contented, in fact that he decided to send his men into battle alone. It was the season for the kingdom's latest conquest, and kings would traditionally accompany their army on the battlefield. But this time, the king decided to stay home. A seemingly insignificant decision, yet one that had life-long consequences.

This king had chosen a path contrary to his calling. In his boredom, he wandered the rooftops of the palace. Overlooking his vast kingdom, he noticed something that night. He saw a beautiful woman. She was bathing. He looked upon her. His gaze led straight to his heart and the fire of his passion was ignited. He called for his servant to seek out this divine creature. The lust in his heart gave way to the sin of his body. This king had taken another man's wife.

The result of the adulterous union was a pregnancy. Because the king's sin would soon be discovered, he devised a plan. The woman's husband was a commander on the battlefield. The king decided to call the woman's husband home from the battle. So, the soldier was given temporary leave and sent home. Surely after weeks on the battlefield, the soldier would be anxious to spend the night with his beautiful wife. Yet the soldier's honor overtook his desire for his wife, and he chose to spend the night at the city gate. If his men could not be home with their wives, he would not go home to his.

The kings' attempt to cover up his sin had failed. He devised a new plan. He sent orders to the battle, that when the soldier returned to the field, he was to be placed in the fiercest conflict; the hot-bed of the battle. His death was certain. The soldier, obedient to his king, gave his life for the kingdom.

The king had succeeded. He had covered his sin. No one would know what he had done.

But there was One who knew. The One who knew everything. The One who sees all things. The One who knows the secrets of the darkness. The One who knew the king's actions. The One who understood the very depths of the king's sinful heart.

This story is an illustration of what an impure heart can look like. It is also a picture of what impurity can do to a family. The focus of this week's study is how to [re]build a strong family and [re]marriage. Be open and honest before Him as we look at what it means to be "pure in heart."

Day One

Put Your Heart Right

"You're blessed when you get your inside world – your mind and heart – put right. Then you can see God in the outside world." Matthew 5:8 (The Message)

You will all likely recognize the story you just read. It is the story of King David and his adulterous affair with the beautiful Bathsheba as recorded in *2 Samuel 11-12*. While David had spent a lifetime living obediently, he had become complacent. Perhaps his role as king had gone to his head. Maybe he thought he was above temptation. But in the midst of his success as a king, David fell. And he fell hard.

As we read the story, we might be thinking that David's actions are unrecoverable. Even today, we see Godly people fall. Sometimes they don't get up. Sometimes they don't recover. And we would likely be tempted to think the same thing of David. After all, he had broken the "biggies" when it comes to the Ten Commandments. He had coveted his neighbor's wife, committed adultery, lied and committed murder. Those are probably the top four worst, right?

But as we continue to learn about what happened in David's life, I want you to observe the truth of restoration. Remember, this week we are looking at what it means to be blessed because of a pure heart. I want you to understand what Jesus means when He talks about purity.

As you probably recall, David did indeed suffer consequences for his sin. The child that was conceived that night, died. Nathan the prophet went to David and told him the story of wealthy man who owned many cattle and sheep. There was a poor man who only had one little ewe lamb. He loved that lamb. It was more like a pet than livestock. A hungry traveler came to town and went to the wealthy man's house and asked for food. Instead of taking one of his own animals from his vast flock to slaughter and provide food for the traveler, the wealthy man stole the little ewe lamb from the poor man and fed it to the traveler.

When David heard this story, he was furious at the wealthy man. He told Nathan, *"As surely as the Lord lives, the man who did this deserves to die! He must pay for that lamb four times over, because he did such a thing and had no pity"* 2 Samuel 12:5-6.

Of course, we know that David is the wealthy man in the story and the ewe lamb that he took was Uriah's wife, Bathsheba. While Nathan went on to tell David that his life would be spared, he also prophesied that the child would die. And because David had sent Uriah to his death in the battle, Nathan told King David that the sword would never depart from his house.

David did take Bathsheba to be his wife. He did lose his son. His household was filled with calamity from that point forward. King David's sin certainly did have consequences. But, God was not finished. There was restoration in David's future.

You may be wondering what this story has to do with being pure in heart and seeing God. Bear with me as we discover what God did for King David. As you know, King David wrote many of the Psalms. One of the most famous Psalms was penned after his fall. His remorse and repentant heart was laid bare in *Psalm 51*. I want us to look at that passage today. Having a pure heart is not something we can conjure up on our own. We can no more purify our own heart than we can pay our own sin debt. God is the only one who can bring purity to a sinful heart.

🐾 *Read Psalm 51.*

Record everything David asks God to do.

What do you learn from *Psalm 51:6*?

What do you learn from *Psalm 51:5*?

What does *Psalm 51:10* say about the heart?

This chapter is full of encouragement to the sinner. I think there are four things we learn about having a pure heart. Consider how these things can apply to you and your family.

God is merciful. Remember when we talked about the difference between grace and mercy? Mercy is when we don't get what we deserve. Surely, David deserved to die for his sin. Yet, God showed mercy. And God's mercy did not depend on David, but was based solely on God's character. God's unfailing love and His great compassion allowed God to be merciful. As God is merciful to you, allow His unfailing love and great compassion to flow through you to others.

Our sin is always against God, not just another person. David recognized that his greatest downfall was the fact he had sinned against God. When we allow sin to overtake us, we are breaking communion with God. While people will suffer because of our sin, God is the One whose standard we have broken. His is the law we have transgressed by our sin.

We are sinful by nature. No one really wants to be sinful. Yet, when Adam and Eve chose to allow evil to enter the garden, sin became resident within the heart of mankind. We are born as a sinner. Think about it. How many of you had to teach your two-year-old to be self-centered and defiant? Did you teach them how to throw fits and demand their own way? Did you teach your children to speak angry words? Of course not. We were all born with the sin nature alive and well. But, God, in His mercy did not leave us in our sin.

God is the creator of the pure heart. David understood that God was the only One who could heal his hurt and cleanse his heart. He asked for God to restore him. David desired a clean, pure heart. He longed for a steadfast spirit. He wanted to again hear joy and gladness.

A pure heart is not impossible. If it were, Jesus would never have preached the joy of a pure heart. In order for us to have a pure heart, there are two things we must acknowledge. We have an impure heart because of our sin nature, and God is able to purify our heart. David gives us a great example of those two things. He went to God with his sin. He took responsibility for his sin. Then, he trusted God to cleanse him of his sin.

🐾 Reflect on Eugene Peterson's translation of this verse from the Message: *"You're blessed when you get your inside world – your mind and heart – put right. Then you can see God in the outside world."* Consider your family as your outside world. Today, we saw the devastation that can happen in a family when an impure heart steps in. When you have a pure heart, you are able to see God in your outside world including your family.

Consider the following questions and record your thoughts.

What is it that prevents you from seeing God in your family?

What change of heart needs to happen for you to be blessed because of your pure heart?

How will this impact your family?

Think about the members of your family. Consider the things that may be getting in the way of purity. Ask God to show you how to lead the way in being blessed because of your pure heart.

Day Two

A Purified Heart

I hope you gained insight yesterday as we looked into the life of David. Before we move on, I want to remind you that God continued to use David in mighty ways after his great sin. In fact, after the son conceived in sin died, David went to comfort Bathsheba. The result of that encounter was the conception of their son, Solomon, who would succeed David on the throne. God called David "a man after God's own heart." God didn't change that description after David sinned. I hope you are encouraged by the story of David. No matter what you have done, or how grievous your sin, God is the God of forgiveness and restoration. He does not discard the sinner. In fact, some of His greatest work comes on the heels of our greatest downfalls.

David had committed acts out of an impure heart. You may have had an experience in your own life where impurity has entered your heart. You may believe that God has finished with you and can never heal you of the impurity. However, as with King David, God is the God of second chances and new birth. David is a picture of God's amazing power to redeem. You have a brand new opportunity for God's blessing in your blending family.

Let's return to the mountain and pick up where we left off. Jesus' entire discourse in this sermon has to do with the contrast between grace and works. While a pillar of the Jewish belief taught works-based salvation by keeping the law, Jesus came along and said that the law existed in order to magnify man's dependence on God which ultimately resulted in His grace. No matter how "good" we are, we can never be "good enough" to earn our own salvation. It is only through the gift of grace we are saved.

Jesus wanted us to understand we could never purify our own hearts, but only God could create within us a pure a heart. Further, Jesus contrasted the state of our heart with the actions of our feet. While we can pretend to be pure, it is only what is in our heart that truly reveals our purity.

How would our life look if we allowed a heart purified by the blood of Jesus to rule our thoughts, words and actions? Would we speak to people differently? Would our attitudes toward those who wrong us be different? Would we make different choices in how we spend our time?

God has given us an opportunity to be more like Him. As we experience a new phase of life as a blending family, we have the opportunity to love someone else's children. Not because we are forced to, but because we choose to. We have the opportunity to show them how Jesus loves. He doesn't love us more if we are good or nice or do what He says. He loves us just because we are His. And He has chosen us to be His. We were not "born" into His family, but He adopted us as family.

Here is what Paul writes to the Ephesian church: *"For He (God) chose us in Him before the creation of the world to be holy and blameless in His sight. In love He predestined us to be **adopted as His sons through Jesus Christ**, in accordance with His pleasure and will..."* Ephesians 1:4-5 *(emphasis mine).* While we won't dive into a discussion on predestination, we do read that Paul reminded the Ephesians we are adopted as God's very own through His only Son, Jesus.

Literally, God gives us a change of heart when we accept the grace of Christ. This change of heart can change the way we live if we allow it. We can begin to live and act and speak as Jesus would. Our lives can be examples of God's grace. Our actions can be generous and focused on others. Our words can be kind and forgiving. Our thoughts can be focused on holiness and righteousness. Let's look at a passage in Psalms to provide practical insight into how to live a life that exemplifies a pure heart.

📖 *Read Psalm 119:9-11.*

How can we remain pure?

There is one common thread. A pure heart is linked to God's Word. Let's consider some ways to live out this principle.

Live according to God's Word. God's Word is a guide to life. When you have a question about the purity of something you are considering, God's Word can give you direction. Let the Word be a guide in directing your steps and actions. Let your family see you sifting your actions and plans through the Word of God.

Seek God with all your heart. This verse ends with the request for God to not let us stray from His commands. His commands are found in His Word. Once again, we see God's reminder that He wants **all** of our heart. Think of it like this. You have just gotten a cup of coffee. You have filled the cup to the very brim. There is not room in the cup for cream or sugar. You can't even drop in an ice cube to cool it down without sending the contents spilling over the brim of the cup. Think of your heart in the same way. God desires to completely fill your heart. If He has filled it completely, there is no room for anything else. Only Him.

Hide God's Word in your heart. This is a very practical application for filling up your heart with God. His Word keeps us from sin. His Word is a lamp to our feet and a light to our path. His Word is the Sword of the Spirit when we are doing battle with the enemy.

When God's Word fills your heart, you are armed and ready to fight the sin that will certainly come before you. I think God is telling us to memorize scripture. I know I sound like your 3rd grade Sunday School teacher, but she was right. Putting God's Word in your head is the first step in getting His Word into your heart. Memorize scripture. Have a plan. Be consistent. Put God's Word in your heart. You'll be surprised at what will pop into your head when temptation comes. It is really hard to walk contrary to God's way when His

Word is speaking in your head. I have a friend who had a monthly family challenge. As their children got older, they chose a whole chapter of the Bible to memorize. If your children are younger, maybe you just want to memorize a verse or two at a time. But the younger they are, the better. Begin early to pour God's Word into them. Fill them up with Him before the world gets a chance. Your children are empty vessels just waiting to be filled. Beat the enemy to the punch. Put so much of God's Word in them when they are young, that when they are older, there is no room for the enemy and his lies.

God's Word not only helps prevent you from giving in to the temptation from sin, but it also acts as a guide. It illumines each step of your journey. It also provides direction. His Word will help you determine the path that is best for you. One of my favorite passages is *Jeremiah 29:11: "'For I know the plans I have for you,' declares the Lord, 'plans to prosper you and not to harm you, plans to give you hope and a future.'"* God has a plan for your life. And His plan is the best plan. Learn His Word and seek His direction.

Finally, Paul tells us in *Ephesians 6:10-18* that we are in a battle. And the battle has nothing to do with how things appear. The real battle is happening in a spirit world we cannot see. The forces of the heavenly realms and forces of the evil one are entrenched in a war. While we can't see it, we are a part of it. Paul says we have battle armor to wear every single day. If you read about the armor, what you will find is that every piece of armor is defensive. Every piece is provided to protect us. Every piece except one. The Sword of Spirit is the only offensive weapon we have. And the Sword of the Spirit is the Word of God.

I came to understand the power of the sword while watching a documentary on the making of a movie set in medieval times. The actors used authentic swords in this movie and were being interviewed about learning to use these impressive weapons. One actor revealed that he had to spend months in the gym lifting weights before he even began training in how to wield the weapon, due to the incredible weight of the sword. These men spent months and months in intensive training before they were able to even learn the choreography of the sword fighting scenes. I realized then what Paul was talking about when he discussed the Sword of the Spirit.

The actors who spent months learning how to use the sword were not even being schooled in life or death fighting. They were simply learning a technique to make a sword fight look authentic. No one's life depended on how skilled they were as a swordsman. We, however, are involved in a real battle every single day. I am challenged. You are challenged.

How skilled are you when called upon to use the Sword?

Are you strong enough to lift the heavy weight of the weapon? Do you know and understand how to wield the weapon with skill and accuracy?

How much time do you spend learning how to use the weapon?

What are some areas you believe Satan may be attacking your purity?

What are some areas your believe Satan may be attacking the purity of your family?

How can you effectively wield the Sword of the Spirit in those attacks?

Accurately using scripture is vital when doing battle against the enemy. Use a good Bible concordance as a tool for finding scripture to pray against the attacks of the enemy. If you are serious about being blessed because of your pure heart, you must understand that a pure heart is rooted in God's Word. Without the purity of God's Word filling your heart, you are open to the impurities of the world and the enemy. Spend time in prayer for you and your family that God would protect you and teach you how to more effectively use the Sword! You have persevered well today. More tomorrow.

Day Three

The Root of David's Sin

Where does a pure heart get off course? What is it that brings impurity into our heart? I want to return to King David for an explanation and practical application. When we really study what happened in King David's life, we learn a lot about how to avoid falling into temptation. We talked at length earlier this week about what David did and how it resulted in an impure heart. Today, I want us to wrestle with where it all started.

📖 **Read Romans 12:1-2.**

What does Paul tells us to do with our bodies?

What does Paul tell us **not** to do?

What does Paul tell us **to do**?

What is the result of the transformation?

I know you must be scratching your head, wondering what all this has to do with David. Stay tuned and I promise this will all fit. Paul writes the Roman church and challenges them. Remember, the Jewish leaders were all about works. Paul spent much of his ink trying to convince the early church that Jesus is the only way to heaven. The path to heaven is not paved with our works. However, he was also quick to tell his readers that works could not be ignored. This passage is a great example.

Paul capitalized on the Jewish understanding of sacrifice. For centuries, their sin had been forgiven as the result of regular animal sacrifices. Paul uses this example to put our works in perspective. There is no longer the need for a dead sacrifice. Christ's death on the cross satisfied the law's demand for a sin sacrifice to pay our sin debt forever. However,

Paul tells us that now what God wants is for us to be living sacrifices. In other words, give yourself completely to God. Live a life that is completely surrendered to Him. This is what is holy and pleasing to God.

Then he goes on to explain how we can do that. Paul knows the natural temptation is to look at the world, and pattern our thoughts, attitudes and actions after it. But Paul encourages us not to be conformed to the world. Instead, he says we are to be transformed. And where is this transformation born? We begin the transformation of our lives by transforming how we think. Paul's words are *"by the renewing of our minds."*

If you really look at what happened to David, you will see that the sins he committed really started with a thought. Remember the story at the beginning of the week? David was walking around the rooftops of the palace, when he saw a beautiful woman. I really don't think David was looking for sin that night. But his eyes saw something beautiful and appealing. Next, his mind responded to his longing. Had David done something different with his *thoughts*, perhaps he never would have sinned.

Our minds are powerful things. I would conjecture that what you do with your thoughts not only impacts your actions, but also reflects the purity of your heart. So how do you go about renewing your mind? Paul has a solution for that as well.

🐾 *Read Philippians 4:8.*

Record the list of things that Paul tells us to think about.

There it is. A litmus test for our thoughts. When an impure thought comes into your mind, and it will, what you do next determines whether or not your heart remains pure. You have the power of the Holy Spirit to help you. Once you have determined the thought is impure and will cause you to sin, give it to God. He is all-powerful to take any thought you release to Him. He is able to replace the evil thought with a pure thought.

As a parent, this is probably one of the most powerful lessons you can teach your children. We are bombarded all day, every day with the enemy and with evil. If you can teach your children how to commit their thought-life to God, you have given them a valuable tool in combatting evil.

Habitual sin that cripples so many, began with a thought. Help your children understand the power they have to overcome evil with good. One of the first verses I remember teaching my preschool-age boys was, *"Do not be overcome by evil, but overcome evil with good."* We even had a song that helped them learn that verse.

As a family, memorize *Philippians 4:8*. Put the words on the refrigerator. Place them on the bathroom mirror. Write the verse on a post-it and put it on the screen of your computers and television sets. Place the words next to the door so that's the last thing you see when you leave your house.

❧ One more thing. Spend some time reflecting on each of these words. Beside each one, write down anything that is keeping you from "thinking" on that particular attribute. Draw a line through what you have written to remind yourself to "cross it out" of your thoughts. Then, record something you could think about that would illustrate the attribute. Pray each of these attributes for your family.

True:

Noble:

Right:

Pure:

Lovely:

Admirable:

Excellent:

Praiseworthy:

Ask God to guard the thoughts of each member of your family. Specifically pray these mental attributes over each family member. As we close, I want to encourage you to spend some time and meditate on this verse: *"Greater is He that is in you, than he that is in the world." 1 John 4:4 (NASB)*

Day Four

Being Transformed

Yesterday we looked at *Romans 12:1-2*. I hope you gleaned valuable truths about the power of your thoughts. I trust you are challenged to intentionally teach your children to give God the reins when it comes to their thoughts. As we continue to focus on being pure in heart, I want to revisit the passage in Romans. There is another valuable truth for us to explore.

🐚 *Reread Romans 12:1-2.*

Romans 12:1-2 challenges us not to conform to the world. Obviously that is a temptation or Paul would not have addressed it. But one thing I love about God's Word is that it never just leaves us with empty "don't's." There is always a Godly or positive replacement for that which God wants to excise. When God tells us not to be afraid, He doesn't just want to remove the fear and leave a giant hole. He wants to take out the fear in order to make a place for His unfathomable peace. When he tells us not to doubt, He doesn't just leave us empty, but He fills that void with His hope.

So when Paul tells us not to conform to the world, he doesn't just leave us there wondering what we are to do instead. He immediately gives us the antidote to conformity. Instead, Paul says, be transformed by the renewing of the mind. He not only gives us the positive, Godly attribute (transformation) but he even tells us how to achieve it. We talked yesterday about the renewing of our minds. Today, I want us to look at what Paul means when he talks about transformation.

In the original language, this word, transformation, can be best described by our English word metamorphosis. Some of you are trying to remember back to elementary school, which is probably the last time you heard this word. Let me help jog your memory. The definition of the word is "a profound change in form from one stage to the next in the life history of an organism."[2] The example we probably all observed as children was the transformation of a caterpillar into a butterfly.

This is a great example to give us a picture of what Paul is teaching. Consider what happens in the world of biology. Think about the caterpillar. His existence is limited to where he can crawl. His days are filled looking for leaves to eat. His perspective of the world is very small. After all he spends his life on his belly.

Then, one day, he suddenly finds himself enveloped in darkness. Something unknown surrounds him. He no longer crawls. He is captive in his small, dark, cramped cell. While trapped, he begins a transformation that he does not control. He begins to change, but doesn't understand nor initiate the change. He is experiencing his transformation.

Finally, an amazing thing happens. He begins to move and struggle. The prison surrounding him becomes brittle. As he moves and works, he realizes there is light piercing his dark cocoon. The more he struggles, the more he longs to be free. Then finally, he is able to break out of his chains. He realizes he is no longer bound to crawl around on his belly. He now has wings. And they are beautiful wings, carrying him high into the sky. He sees the world from the tops of the trees. He is free in a way he has never before known. The lowly caterpillar has been transformed into a beautiful butterfly.

I hope as you were reading, you were thinking of your own journey of transformation. The story of the butterfly is one that beautifully illustrates the transformation God desires to work in our lives. As you think about the transformation God desires, think beyond yourself. Yes, He is doing a work personally. But what is the transformation He wants to bring to your family? Consider the application of this passage to your family. Here are a few suggestions.

Consider where your family falls on the transformation scale. No matter how long you have been a family, think about how far you have come. Are you still crawling around trying to find something to eat? The caterpillar has to fill up on leaves before he is ready to enter the cocoon. Caterpillars are in a season of preparation for what is to come. Your family may still be in the preparation mode. If so, do what you need to do in order to prepare. Are there fractured relationships? Perhaps it's time to forgive and move forward. Maybe there is some work you need to do to regarding forgiveness in your previous marriage. Perhaps mercy is your starting place for transformation.

Your family may be in the darkness of the cocoon. There is much work God does during this stage of metamorphosis. While this is not a science lesson, think about what the pupa does while in the cocoon. He is simply waiting on God to do the work. If your family is in this stage, consider the work God is doing.

Perhaps this is a good time to interject some important principles from the world of team-building. Bruce Tuckman first introduced the Tuckman Model for team building in 1965[3]. Many workshops still teach these principles as organizations come together. While you are a family, not a business, this might provide insight into where your family falls on the transformation scale.

Form. The first stage of any new team requires they first form. Obviously. A random group of folks come together to make a team. Hopefully they share similar goals and visions for the organization. They may not know one another very well, but each brings a unique set of skills, strengths, weaknesses, and previous experiences to the table.

Storm. Stage two of the team formation usually sees the individual personalities coming out and trying to figure each other out, and how to most effectively work together. Leadership experts and team-building gurus will tell you, while it may be uncomfortable and stressful, this stage is essential to forming a healthy and productive team. Struggles between team members are inevitable and essential to get to the next stage of team development.

Norm. As the struggles subside and team members begin to understand, appreciate and even value their differences, a set of normative behaviors within the team are established. Everyone on the team learns their unique role, and how they can best work with other team members.

Perform. The final stage gives birth to the effective performance of the team. They have figured out how to work together, encourage each other, tolerate the differences among the members and function productively.

🕮 Identify the current stage of your family. How is God working on your family in this stage? What does He want you to learn?

Trust God in the stage. Allow Him to work. As a family, are you willing to be molded and transformed? While the molding may be painful, keep your eye on the outcome.

Trust God with the struggles as your family is transforming. If you are coming out of the cocoon, here is something important to know. When I was a little girl, we collected what we called "hairy worms." They were actually caterpillars. But they were brown and hairy. We would catch them in a jar, punch holes in the jar lid, stick some grass and leaves in the jar, and drip some water in as well. Over time, the cocoon would appear. Then, after waiting what seemed an eternity, we would see the butterfly begin to emerge. I learned a valuable lesson with one of our Hairys.

Hairy was beginning to emerge from his shell. He was struggling and working and laboring to break free of the cocoon. I really felt sorry for him. He was working so hard to get out. My merciful heart got the best of me and I decided to help him out a little bit. I gently pulled on a wing and broke away a part of the cocoon. He was finally free. But he stayed in the jar. He would not come out. I finally turned the jar over and dumped him out on the grass. I thought surely he would fly away. But he didn't. Because he couldn't. In my zeal to make things easier for him to release himself from the cocoon, I had actually prevented him from being able to do what he was created to do. In order for their wings to be strong enough to fly, the emerging butterfly must struggle on their own to get out of the cocoon.

Your family may be struggling to release themselves from the cocoon. If so, don't try to prevent the struggle, but trust God with it. It is often through difficulty that we experience God more fully. Be wise in how you lead your family through their transformation. There are no short cuts. Remember, it is often through the struggles that we are strengthened for the journey ahead. Without the struggle to get out of the cocoon, the butterfly's wings are not strong enough to soar.

🕮 **Read Romans 5:3-5**

What does this passage teach us about struggles and transformation?

Allow your family to soar! Finally, if your family is soaring, rejoice! Think of the freedom the once-bound butterfly must feel when finally able to fly. The temptation for your family may be to return to the ground. Sometimes struggles and trials rob us of the joy and freedom we have in Christ. If you have become temporarily derailed as a family, go back to the moment when God released you from your cocoon. Remember who He has created you to be as a family, and reclaim the joy you found in flight.

Read Isaiah 40:31.

What application do you find in this passage as it speaks to your family soaring?

Spend some time with your spouse and your family discussing what God is doing in your family. Talk about where your family falls in their transformation. Listen to the hearts of your children as they evaluate your family's transformation. Spend time praying as a family. Lead your family to trust God as He molds your family according to His plan and His purpose.

If you have younger children, you might want to catch a caterpillar and let them watch the process of metamorphosis. This picture from the world of biology gives you great opportunities to draw significant parallels with the life of the believer and the transformation God is bringing about in your family.

Day Five

From the Inside Out

We have seen throughout this study on purity that God's primary focus is on the heart of man. The actions are not the focus. Actions are simply the result of a heart longing to follow God. The Jewish religious leaders had things backwards. They wanted to believe that righteous actions would purify their hearts. Yet Jesus called them *whitewashed tombs (Matthew 23:27)*. Inside was death and darkness; the stench of decay and the complete absence of life. Yet, paint the sepulcher with bright, white paint, hang a sprig of lavender in front of the stone, and no one really knows what lies inside.

Jesus comes along and turns the world upside down. Or should I say, inside out. Jesus taught what God is most concerned about is found on the inside. We can make ourselves look good on the outside all day. But at the end of the day, when everything is stripped away, and it's just us and God, our true identity surfaces. Who we are on the inside becomes clear.

Jesus says, at the heart of the matter, if we are pure we will see God. I don't think He means God will appear in a vision. Of course, He could if He chose to. He's God. He can do anything He pleases. But I think the principle Jesus was teaching was more about our worldview. I think He is teaching if our heart is pure, we are able to see the world, and other people the way God sees them. Then, we are better able to treat others the way God wants us to treat them.

Consider how you can view your family through God's eyes. Allow Him to purify your heart and open your eyes to the needs and struggles of those in your family. Resolve to be an agent of healing and encouragement to each member of your family. Commit to allow God to rule in your heart and keep you pure.

I hope you will allow me a moment of honest concern. Over the last few years, my job had led me to minister in the world of human trafficking, the sex industry and pornography. The things I've learned have been overwhelming, and honestly somewhat devastating. While I live in what I thought was a clean, whitewashed suburb, I always considered those things to be dark and seedy and very far away from me. But I have learned differently. They are very dark and very dangerous. They are truly destructive to lives and to families. But they are not far away from me. Human trafficking happens everywhere. If you think your community is immune, I challenge you to contact your local police department and ask. Sex and labor trafficking is pervasive. It is everywhere. Even in our nice, clean, quiet, family neighborhoods.

Along the same lines, while conducting research for a project a couple of years ago, I was confronted with the epidemic of pornography. I was completely taken off guard by the statistics I found. One statistic I uncovered reports that 50% of the men and 20% of the women who are **practicing Christians, active in evangelical churches, struggle with**

pornography[4]. My heart has been broken for the families I've met who have been destroyed because of pornography. If you or someone in your family struggles with pornography, let today be the day you find help. Jay Dennis, pastor of Church on the Mall in Lakeland, Florida has written a book challenging men to live pornography free. You can get information at Jay's website join1millionmen.org. As wives and mothers, I challenge you to pray for all the men in your life that they may remain porn free. Pornography cannot be controlled. It is as addictive as crack cocaine. It is destroying families. If you have an issue in your family with anyone who is viewing pornography, please, seek professional help.

Thank you for allowing me to share my heart. I know this is a tough subject, but the enemy is using it in powerful ways to destroy our families. Don't let your family be a casualty. There is help and hope through the power of the Holy Spirit. Spend time in prayer for your family. Ask God to provide a covering over everyone in your home. Ask Him to help you be wise as you guard what your children see and have access to on television and the internet. Be proactive to protect those in your home from the devastation Satan desires from an impure heart.

As we close out this week, allow me to completely switch gears. Your head may still be spinning from reading the previous paragraph. But I do want to address a blending family subject that comes up frequently in our conversations and surveys. It doesn't necessarily relate with the beatitude we are discussing, but perhaps we can make a few connections.

When two families come together to blend, there are a variety of things that have to be blended. The obvious things involve the combination of households. Decisions must be made about what is to be kept and what is to be discarded. After all, who needs four sofas, two dining tables, two kitchen tables and twelve televisions?

As you have grown together as a family you have likely found other, less tangible things that have required some negotiation. Many blending families come to blows over family traditions, especially as they relate to the holidays. Honestly, there are no easy answers. But just like you worked through whose dining table to keep, and which televisions to sell, you will also have the opportunity to talk through family traditions.

As you consider your new family's traditions, evaluate what they say about your faith priorities. One of the most difficult things blending families can encounter is the rebuilding of family traditions. The family members have come out of other families who have established traditions. It may no longer be appropriate to hold to the past traditions. You now have the challenge, or maybe we could call it an opportunity, to start new ones. Some things may need to be carefully addressed, but coming together as a couple, then including children in the discussion can give everyone a chance to speak into the process. But just remember, as you are establishing new patterns and traditions for your blending family, allow God's teaching to guide your choices. And you can use this opportunity to tell your children why you are making some of the choices you are.

What about holidays? At the risk of seeming crude, our kids often referred to the "f" word in our home. Before you panic, let me elaborate. Our new blending family's buzz word quickly became *flexibility*. To the point that our children hated that word. It seemed that every time we turned around, we were asking them to just be flexible. The kids had grown so weary of the concept they simply began to refer to it as the "f" word. But with regard to holidays, flexibility is critical. Here are a few practical suggestions as you work to rebuild family and holiday traditions.

Focus on creating memories rather than keeping traditions alive. It's tough enough to hang onto tradition in a nuclear family. But once you begin to consider all the surrounding people that now have influence on your family, establishing traditions may seem impossible. Let me challenge you to consider what it is about holiday traditions that is actually important? I know we would all like to be together as a family every single Christmas morning forever, but the reality is that although not impossible, that is highly unlikely. So how do you manage the lack of tradition? Perhaps the lack of tradition is the tradition. After all, the significance of holiday tradition is to create memories. So when things can't be exactly as you would like them to be, how you choose to respond is creating a memory. Will your children remember you being angry and defiant when things don't go according to your tradition, or will they see grace in action as you enjoy the true meaning of family regardless of how, when or where you gather?

Capture the moment … whenever it is. We westerners tend to be major planners. We map out everything from family gatherings to daily chores to weekly agendas. While not altogether bad, sometimes we miss out on some special moments because they just happen to be spontaneous, outside of our plan. There is a really fun word that I've come to cherish. Serendipity. I like it because it sounds like what it actually is. The word means a fortunate discovery by accident; fortunate happenstance; pleasant surprise. I actually like to look for serendipities throughout the day. You have the same opportunity. Some of my most cherished memories with my family are serendipitous. Completely unplanned, completely unexpected, but an incredible blessing or memory. Just because it isn't in your plan, be willing to embrace the unexpected.

Laughter is the best medicine. Did you know this is actually found in Proverbs? *"A cheerful heart is good medicine, but a crushed spirit dries up the bones" Proverbs 17:22.* While we may feel like crying more times than not, why not try approaching life with a cheerful heart? I'm amazed how quickly my perspective lightens when I choose to laugh. There is a reason that funny videos online go viral so quickly. I think people are hungry to laugh. Life is heavy. Life is hard. So maybe if we choose to laugh, we can begin to develop an atmosphere of joy in our home. Let laughter pick up the spirit in your home.

Is your head spinning? We have discussed pornography and holiday traditions within the same day's study. How are they linked, and how do they relate to blending families? Remember, this week's study is about purity within your [re]marriage and stepfamily. Too often we set our new families up for failure because we focus on circumstance rather than people. Doing so will create dissention every time. A lack of purity in your [re]marriage can result in wandering eyes and self-pleasure via pornography or affairs. A lack of purity through selfish desires via "my way or the highway," when it comes to family traditions, can also divide and defeat your family.

Perhaps the study this week has been challenging. As you consider being blessed because of your pure heart, resolve to trust God to help you keep it that way. See God in the things around you and look for Him as He desires to work through you and your family.

Week Seven

Make Peace

"Blessed are the peacemakers for they will be called the sons of God." Matthew 5:9

An interesting thing happens in families when they become blended. Birth order changes. In our home, my youngest suddenly became a middle child. My husband's oldest became another middle child. My oldest remained the oldest, and his youngest remained the baby. At least until we had a child together. An interesting observation from our blending family, is that the oldest and the youngest seemed to manage the transition fairly well. Part of that could have been their even temperaments. Even so, the middle two were the ones who seemed to have the hardest time blending. They are very close in age, and very similar in personality. Both out-going and open. They spoke without filters and everyone in the house knew how they felt as soon as they walked in the door.

Early in our blending process, we began to have family devotional times together. The age range for the kids was 3-years-old to 10-years-old, so we had to be creative to keep everyone engaged. Our family was a little over a year old, and we were in the midst of a family devotional. I can't tell you what the topic was, nor what the activities included, but I do remember the explosion. Something prompted a heated verbal exchange between the two middle kids. I remember sitting in the chair, stunned at the flood of emotions landing in the living room floor. At that moment, those two could not stand the sight of each other. Immediately, our family devotional topic changed.

After getting everyone calmed down, and letting the kids say what they needed to say, my husband decided to take those two on a walk, with just the three of them. The kids needed to expend some energy to help the anger reach a manageable level.

We lived in a beautiful neighborhood, full of large, mature trees, a golf course and some small bodies of water. As you might expect, seeing a snake or two would not be unusual. Now in my world, a snake is nothing but the embodiment of evil and there is nothing more upsetting to me than encountering one. But I trust in Almighty God who made them and I know He can use all things, even those nasty snakes, to do a work. And that is exactly what He did. As the three were walking along the sidewalk, there it was. A snake right in front of them. The anger became fear, the walk became a sprint, and by the time the three of them were back at home, all I could hear was laughter bursting through the front door. What had started as a war, had somehow melted into peace.

Peace is a difficult thing to manufacture. Heads of countries can't seem to figure it out. Schools can't seem to figure it out. Communities can't seem to figure it out. Many times, even churches can't figure it out. So when our families are in turmoil, we are in good company. While peace on the outside seems illusive, we have great news from Jesus. Although He assures us we will have trouble in this world, He also promises His peace. And His peace is not like the peace the world gives.

In your home, you will have conflict. And the peace God wants for you in the midst of the conflict isn't like the world's peace. It isn't a treaty signed reluctantly by two unwilling parties, providing only surface peace. The peace we have through Christ comes from within. On the outside, the war in your home may seem impossible to end. But the peace we can experience from within, will allow the conflict to be an opportunity for coming together.

So as we begin to look at this beatitude, remember the peace Christ gives comes through the power of the Holy Spirit. Before we even begin our study this week, I encourage you to start now praying God's peace over your household, and every member in it. You'll be amazed at what God will do.

Day One

The Challenge

"You're blessed when you can show people how to cooperate instead of compete or fight. That's when you discover who you really are, and your place in God's family." Matthew 5:9 (The Message)

Are you a peacemaker? God has given you many opportunities to grow and develop your peacemaking muscles if you are in a blending family. You encounter many challenges. You may have an ex-spouse who provides the opportunity for you to be the peacemaker. You have a house full of children who need you to be a peacemaker. You have a new spouse who may long for you to be the peacemaker. But how can you do it? Jesus says, *"Blessed are the peacemakers, for they will be called sons of God."*

Before we can ever begin to make peace with others, we must first make peace with God. It is through the work of the Holy Spirit in us that gives us the power to be a peacemaker. First, make sure you are at peace with your heavenly Father. Once you are at peace with God, the work of His Spirit is unleashed in you.

With that being said, it may still be difficult to be the peacemaker. Sometimes I want to add parentheses to some of Jesus' statements. For instance, I would like to add that Jesus had some exceptions to the peacemaking. We are peacemakers as long as others are able to make peace with us. I'm wondering if he could have made an exception here for our ex-spouses or maybe some of the people in our new family.

But Jesus made no exception. He didn't make this statement conditional upon how the other person or people behave. He has said that if we can be the peacemaker, we are called sons of God.

🐾 Are you able to be the peacemaker in your family because you are at peace with how God is transforming your heart and life? If not, what are your obstacles?

As we look at what it means to be a peacemaker, perhaps we need to look at what the word "peace" actually means in God's economy. When we hear the word "peace," I'm sure it conjures images, ideas or ideals in our mind. In our world, our leaders are constantly working to establish peace among peoples and nations. And this is nothing new. The Old Testament is full of battles and wars where leaders were trying to establish peace with their neighbors and their enemies.

Anyone who grew up in the 1960's-1970's certainly has images of peace signs ... everywhere. Peace signs tie-dyed on t-shirts. Peace signs painted on buildings. Peace signs appliqued on bell-bottom jeans. The irony of those decades was that, in the midst of all those peace signs, peace was nowhere to be found. Peace was an illusion in the world. We were in the throes of a controversial war in Vietnam. Peace was an illusion in our country. We were experiencing unprecedented violence in our country over civil rights. Peace was an illusion in our homes. The younger generation of hippies was at war with their pro-establishment parents. While outwardly we had peace signs everywhere, peace was not a reality anywhere.

Perhaps your blending home today feels something like that. While you would love to emblazon peace signs all over your house, they would only be outward symbols with no real hope of bringing an inward peace. In order to be a peacemaker, we must first understand God's peace.

📖 Read Galatians 5:16-25.

Paul is the author of Galatians and this is actually a letter Paul sent to address some issues the Galatian believers were experiencing. He has some encouragement for them in this passage.

What was Paul contrasting in *Galatians 5:16-17*?

What are the acts of the sinful nature Paul records?

What is the fruit of Spirit Paul notes?

While we could spend pages taking apart this passage, there are a few observations that are helpful to our study. As you look over the list you made of the sinful nature, I encourage you to pause and ask God to show you any area where you may personally struggle. As a Christ-follower, you have the power of the Holy Spirit to overcome anything that comes naturally to your flesh. God longs for you to be an overcomer. He longs to empower you for victory over the sin nature alive in you.

✎ Take a moment to write out the temptations you struggle with. Then, ask God to help you overcome and be empowered to defeat the sin nature in your life.

Now look at the list you made for the fruit of the Spirit. When you were indwelt with the Holy Spirit, this is the nature that became a part of you. The peace you have available to you has the power of God behind it. You carry His very nature of peace within you.

In *John 14:27*, Jesus gives us an insight into the kind of peace we have through Him. He says, *"Peace I leave with you; my peace I give you. I do not give to you as the world gives. Do not let your hearts be troubled and do not be afraid."* Jesus explains to His disciples that through the coming Holy Spirit, they will have access to His peace. He contrasts God's peace with the peace of the world. The world's peace is external, surface and temporary. But God's peace is within us. We can have peace internally, regardless of what's happening around us. God's peace transcends the world. Therefore, our hearts have no need to be troubled, because we have nothing to fear.

So what does this have to do with being a peacemaker in what may have become the warzone of your blending family? On the surface, your conflicts may seem unresolvable. There may be ongoing skirmishes, or even an all-out war between stepsiblings. There may be a continual battle with an ex-spouse. You may find yourself at war with your spouse. You have tried everything to bring peace. You have tried to have everyone sign peace treaties. You have asked for a truce. And, honestly, right now you would be happy with a simple cease-fire. Yet nothing seems to work.

Maybe you will find some encouragement in knowing every member of your household who is a Christ-follower, has the peace of the Holy Spirit already in them. So how do you encourage them to act in peace? First, never underestimate the power of prayer. Pray for God's Spirit to completely take over in the hearts and minds of everyone in your family.

Let me invite you to try something. When all of our children were still at home, there were times, actually seasons of time when things just seemed to be anything but peaceful. I could almost feel a sense of conflict when I walked in the door of our home. I had a friend that had talked about "praying her house." I wasn't sure what that meant, so I talked to her about it one day. While there is nothing magical about what she recommended, I did find her suggestion to be in line with scripture.

So I decided to give it a try. I spent time in prayer, personally, then I walked around our home, inside and out and asked God to bring a spirit of peace in every single room and around the yard. I think, if anything else, it made me more aware of God's presence in and around my family. I know I was personally more aware of my responses and how I related with the people in my family as a result of the "housecleaning." I asked God to remove any spirit of conflict and selfishness. I asked Him to replace those things with His selfless love and supernatural peace.

This can help set the stage for peaceful encounters among family members. However, internal peace sometimes requires some external experiences. When families come together all at once, there are likely feelings that need to be processed. Children are forced into relationships they did not personally choose. Nuclear families introduce new siblings over the course of time. The siblings are introduced as helpless infants. And while the older siblings may not be fond of this new addition, eventually, the family is able to process together, and there is acceptance of the family unit. Even as the children grow and arguments and fights between siblings become common, there is something that happens because the family is biologically nuclear. Somehow, there is freedom and openness to talk things through. Kids find ways to talk through or fight through the issues that divide them and ultimately come to an agreement.

In my mind, I see the picture of two brothers who fight like dogs after the same bone, but when anyone, and I mean anyone even thinks about threatening either of them, the other comes out fighting. They may want to kill each other, while at the same time defending each other to the death if threatened by an outsider.

In stepfamilies, the lines between who is in and who is out become blurred. Overnight, simply because of a couple of "I do's," these kids who were once strangers are now told they are brothers and sisters. No opportunity to get used to the new scenario. They are instantly thrust together and expected to get along. Sometimes, stepsiblings are even required to share a bedroom, losing all sense of autonomy, privacy and control. How can we begin to create peace in such an instance? And for those children who are required to be siblings only on first, third and fifth weekends, it becomes even more difficult to un-blur the lines between who is in and who is out. Allow me to make three suggestions based on scripture.

Be a parent who fears the Lord.

Read Psalm 112. Record everything you learn about the man who fears the Lord.

Here are a couple of things to help clarify this passage. First of all, fear of the Lord does not mean trembling in fright. The Treasury of David states it like this: "Jehovah is so great that he is to be feared and had in reverence of all them that are round about him, and he is at the same time so infinitely good that the fear is sweetened into filial love, and becomes a delightful emotion, by no means engendering bondage. There is a slavish fear which is accursed; but that godly fear which leads to delight in the service of God is infinitely blessed."[5] We are not afraid of God, but we have a deep longing and desire to reverence Him, thus choosing to obey His commands. *Psalm 111:10* says *"The fear of the Lord is the beginning of wisdom ..."* A man is blessed when he understands the power of following God's ways.

If you want to engender security and trust in your children and family, allow it to manifest within you. As you walk in God's ways, you grow in your understanding and wisdom, living in true freedom from fear. Your family is watching you. They see God in you rather than the reaction of the natural man in you.

Assure the children they are secure in their relationship with their biological parents. Notice what the Psalmist says about the children of the man who fears the Lord in *Psalm 112:2*. God spends a fair amount of time throughout scripture exhorting us to follow Him, so that it will go well with our children. The children of the man who fears the Lord *will be mighty in the land and the generation of the upright will be blessed.*

As you walk in the fear of the Lord, your children will be secure in their relationship with you. This relationship is the only security your children have been able to maintain. While they likely long for both parents to live together in harmony, the reality in their life is their sense of security has already been compromised. Throwing them into new relationships with stepsiblings can be overwhelming. Make sure they know you are there for them and you still love them.

Trust in God's wisdom as you counsel your blending children. *"Even in the darkness light dawns for the upright, for the gracious and compassionate and righteous man." Psalm 112:4*

As you begin to parent this blending group of children, you will likely feel as though you are stumbling around in the dark. There are always more questions than answers. There are feelings and frustrations that are new and foreign. There are different perspectives outside of your own previous family's way of thinking. There are hurts and fears beyond what you have dealt with before. Yet, the Psalmist reminds you the light will dawn for the upright. You are even encouraged to be gracious, compassionate and righteous.

Pray for God to help you know how to best comfort and encourage every child who now resides under your roof. As the parent or step-parent, be gracious and compassionate, even when you don't want to. Give the children in your new family the opportunity to share their feelings with you. Listen with grace and compassion. Hear them as children who have lost the most important relationship in their life. They are having to reestablish security without the 24/7 presence of one of their parents. Be willing to listen without judgment and hear with compassion.

As we close our discussion today, spend some time asking God to give you wisdom when it comes to being a peacemaker. The enemy would love nothing more than to maintain a battleground in your new home. Don't give him the victory. Trust the Spirit of peace that is in you. Allow God to grow you into the peacemaker in your family.

🐾 What are some perpetual battles you face in your home? Write them down.

How can you be a peacemaker in the midst of the ongoing battles?

Day Two

How to Have Peace

As you are learning to be a peacemaker, I want to give you another opportunity to learn what God teaches us about peace. Let's look at an additional passage on the subject. It is found in another of Paul's letters. This time, he addresses his beloved Philippian church.

Read Philippians 4:4-7.

What does Paul exhort the Philippians to do?

I find it interesting that Paul is writing this letter from prison. He is telling the Philippians to simply rejoice in the Lord. And when are they to rejoice? When the kids are all getting along, work is a breeze and you and your spouse could just as well be on your honeymoon? Paul says to rejoice *always*. Even when it feels like life is completely falling apart, Paul says to rejoice.

One thing I've learned about rejoicing, is that I have to choose it. That warm feeling of contentment does not often just flood across me and take me away. I have to decide, even though the kids are at each other's throats, work is a nightmare and my spouse is about as far away from me as he can get, I will rejoice. But then, something amazing begins to happen. As I rejoice, my perspective begins to change. As I rejoice, God begins to do a work in my own heart and mind, and I begin to see things through lighter lenses. Things don't seem so heavy and daunting, and I can actually feel the power of God's presence lightening my load. I think there is a verse about that, too. Jesus said, *"Come to me all you who are weary and burdened, and I will give you rest. Take my yoke upon you and learn from me, for I am gentle and humble in heart, and you will find rest for your souls. For my yoke is easy and my burden is light." Matthew 11:28-30.*

What does Paul tell the Philippians in *Philippians 4:5*?

The next word Paul gives his friends in Philippi is that their gentleness should be evident to everyone. How do you deal with your family when peace is the last thing they are experiencing? Do you get caught up in the tornado as well? Paul says gentleness is an important quality to exhibit. But if you are rejoicing, responding in gentleness is an easier choice to make.

In *Philippians 4:6*, what does Paul exhort the Philippians **not** to do?

What is his antidote for worry (or being anxious) in the same verse?

What is the result of this in *Philippians 4:7*?

There is so much in these verses. Let's take them apart piece-by-piece. First of all, Paul speaks of what **not** to do. He tells us **not** to be anxious or worry about anything. That's impossible, you say. Worry is such a natural response. But worry divides our minds. Perhaps that is why Paul is so emphatic. He does not say you shouldn't worry. He does not even say that you are better off if you don't. He simply says just don't do it.

But he does not leave us there in our agony. He gives an alternative. He says worry and anxiety can be a reminder to pray. Paul even elaborates on how to pray. He says we are to be thankful. Thank God that He hears and answers. Thank Him that He is bigger than the worry. Then, Paul tells us to petition God. Literally, to ask Him for what you need. Thank Him for His answer before you ask for what you need. What an interesting way to pray.

Remember, we are looking for peace. How do we find it, according to Paul? Paul says that prayer, not worry will bring us peace. But not just any old peace. God gives us a supernatural peace that transcends our understanding. We don't know how He does it, He just does.

Paul then explains what that kind of peace does for us. *Philippians 4:7* says the peace God gives us will *guard our hearts and minds in Christ Jesus.* The peace isn't just for right now, but the peace God gives us will act as a fortress or garrison over our hearts and minds. Literally, God's peace will protect our hearts and minds from worry in the future. Think of Him surrounding your heart and mind with a solid wall of peace. Nothing can penetrate the fortress.

We can find great encouragement, knowing when Jesus exhorts us to be peacemakers, He is not asking us to do it in our own strength. We have the power of God ready and waiting to be the source of our peace.

Today's lesson is short. I want you to take some time to meditate on the passage we looked at today. It is so powerful, and I want you to consider the truths you have learned, and even begin to commit the passage to memory. Challenge your spouse. Both of you commit to memorize *Philippians 4:4-9.*

I know we only discussed *Philippians 4:4-7* today. You will recall we discussed *Philippians 4:8* in a previous week. It is important to keep these verses in context. As you memorize the list in *Philippians 4:8*, remember what Paul is teaching. He is giving you a litmus test for your thoughts and what you allow your mind to dwell upon. You have choices all throughout the day with regard to your mind. Hebrews says we really can't begin to change our behavior without first getting a handle on our thoughts. It is through the renewing of our minds, that our lives are transformed. If you are able to memorize this list, it will give you ammunition the next time the enemy begins to whisper his lies in your ears.

And finally, Paul closes with the reminder that if you will think on these things, and live your life the way he has modeled as a follower of Christ, you will experience the presence of the God of peace. The next time you feel turmoil and conflict rising up, take a moment to stop your flurry of thoughts, and go to God.

Today, are you skeptical about peace in your home? If so, list your doubts and challenge yourself to determine if any are irrational.

Ask God to remind you of the power of His peace within you. Ask Him to help you become the vessel of peace in your home.

Day Three

Discipline

As we have done research for *family [re]design*, another topic that seems to come up a lot regards disciplining children. Before you think this is only a difficult subject for the blending family, let me help set your mind at ease. Before I was ever a blending family, my bookshelves were full of books written by experts in the area of discipline.

If you have been around a while, you will likely remember that the children's guru of my generation was Dr. Spock. And for you younger folks, he was not on Star Trek. This was a real guy, Dr. Benjamin Spock, who wrote a book that some parents considered the bible of child-rearing.

As the decades passed and other authors came on the scene, we saw the pendulum swing. While Spock would advocate certain types of punishment, the next decade would usher in new ideas. Do spank. Don't spank. Time-outs are good for behavior modification. Time-outs are ineffective in modifying behavior. I remember Dr. T. Berry Brazelton (a pediatrician who spoke wisdom into my generation of parents of infants and toddlers during the 1980's), telling a young mom on a talk show that as long as her son would eat a piece of bread and take vitamin supplements, he would be fine. Don't make him eat. Don't make children clean their plate. But clean your plate because there are so many children who go without. Drink milk. Don't drink milk. Let children have pacifiers to self soothe. Never let a child have a pacifier because they will never learn to self-soothe. Completely confusing.

When I was in the hospital bearing children the first time around, my room was filled with posters reminding mothers to **never** place an infant on their back to sleep. Always side or stomach. I remember going in one afternoon to check on my oldest son who was napping. He had rolled over on his back while sleeping. I absolutely panicked. Should I awaken him to turn him back over or place him on his side? I stood over him to watch and make sure he survived until he woke up.

Then, a decade or so later, I was once again experiencing childbirth. Placed prominently on the wall of the shower in my room was a poster stating **never** place an infant on their stomach. Only on their back or propped up on their side.

So why should we be surprised that step-parenting brings a flood of confusion? If nuclear parenting is hard, how can we begin to get a handle on step-parenting? Before you decide there are no answers, let's look at what the greatest wisdom ever written has to say about parenting.

Recently, God has taken me through a study of Proverbs. Admittedly, I had never really spent a lot of time there. It did not seem like there was much to study. Just a lot of pithy little sayings about life. But when God told me to get serious and look into the wisdom to be found there, I listened and obeyed. I must admit, He did a work in me. I learned so much as I intentionally studied through Proverbs. Now would be a great place to share with you some of the things I learned. While I know we are focusing on making peace in our blending family, bear with me as I share wisdom that I believe will lay the groundwork for an amazingly peaceful home.

Before we begin, let me give you some background so you will understand the context of the book of Proverbs. These sayings were written by King Solomon. He was the King of Israel who followed His father David. He was the product of the union between King David and Bathsheba. As you remember, they had an adulterous affair that resulted in the death of the son of their union. However, after taking Bathsheba as a wife, David went to her to console her after the death of that son. The result of that consolation was the conception of Solomon.

God appeared to King Solomon in a dream and told Solomon to ask whatever he wished, and God would grant it. Instead of asking for wealth or fame, Solomon asked for an understanding heart in order to lead the nation of Israel. (*1 Kings 3*). God granted Solomon *"wisdom and very great discernment and breadth of mind, like the sand that is on the seashore. And Solomon's wisdom surpassed the wisdom of all the sons of the east and all the wisdom of Egypt. For he was wiser than all men. (1 Kings 4:29-32).*

While Solomon spoke over 3,000 proverbs, only a portion of those are recorded in this book of wisdom literature. It is intended as a collection of true sayings which give instruction and wisdom. While they are not prophecies or doctrines, they are a guide by which we are to live.

As we begin our study of wisdom regarding disciplining our children, we will look at *Proverbs 4.* Many proverbs provide instructions to children and give parents wisdom for discipline. This chapter, however, is focused on fathers and sons.

🎵 *Read Proverbs 4.*

Record everything you learn about the instructions of a Father.

Record all the benefits to the son.

Wisdom is often referred to with a feminine pronoun. Record everything you learn about wisdom in the passage.

There is a long list of things we can learn as parents. This chapter gives us a great guide in what to teach our children. You now have a long list of ways to encourage your children to live. But how do you actually teach these things to your children and stepchildren? Here are six suggestions.

Understand what discipline is and what it is not. We tend to interchange the word punishment with discipline. These words are not the same. While God's judgment is certainly experienced through His wrath, His discipline is grounded in His love for us. Punishment has in its etymology the idea of being punitive. Punishment does not have at its heart to be restorative, rather it implies being "treated roughly" for moral infractions. Punishment is really intended to bring pain to the offender with the purpose not of bringing regeneration or real repentance, but simply using pain as an external consequence to prevent the infraction in the future.

Discipline has a completely different intention. Look at the word through the lens of scripture. Jesus had disciples, or those who were disciplined in His truth. The use of discipline with our children brings with it the idea of training or restoration, motivated by love and rooted in the desire to bring a change of heart as well as behavior. The objective of discipline is to bring about growth or development in the one being disciplined. Our discipline is motivated by love for the one undergoing correction.

Punishment has as its goal to simply bring pain as the consequence for an unwanted behavior and is primarily focused on the one bringing the punishment. Discipline has as its goal to restore and bring a change of heart. Its primary focus is on the internal transformation of the offender and is rooted in love.

When correcting children, we must always consider the motive for our reaction to their behavior. With our own biological children we sometimes struggle to regain our emotions before lashing out at them. With our stepchildren, it may be much more difficult to contain our feelings before reacting. This is especially true when tension with the ex-spouse is heightened. Consider these questions to evaluate your motive for discipline.

What is your goal when confronted with a situation where you believe discipline is necessary?

Do you want to get even? Do you want that child to be sorry for the pain they may have caused? Or, do you want to help the child grow in their wisdom and understanding with regard to Godliness?

Should discipline hurt?

My only answer is that when God disciplines me, and He does, it hurts. It brings me to a place where I feel genuine remorse and a longing to ask forgiveness and repent. Before the situation with a stepchild arises, spend time with your mate and discuss your philosophy of discipline. As with your child's other biological parent, there will likely be some disparity in philosophy. Look to God's Word as a guide helping you through the areas of disagreement. Here are some questions to ask as you explore:

Is my philosophy based on God's Word or on my own family's tradition?
Does my philosophy keep the best interest of each child at the forefront?
Does my philosophy focus more on the child or on me?
Does my philosophy violate any of God's principles for living righteously?

Determine each parent's non-negotiables for parenting. As you discuss parenting, each of you will likely have at least a couple of things you are not willing to negotiate. Those need to be clearly stated, understood and respected. There may need to be some extensive discussions if your non-negotiables impact other children in the home. Perhaps you believe in spanking your children and your spouse is vehemently opposed to it. This will require prayer, discussion and perhaps some patience as you work through the issue. If there are children from only one parent, the step-parent will need to accept the decision of the biological parent. The problems arise if children are parented differently in the same home. If both spouses bring children into the home and differ in how they choose to parent, issues can arise not only between spouses, but between stepsiblings as well as step-parents and stepchildren. As you individually soul-search for why you choose to parent as you do, perhaps a few words of wisdom will help.

🕮 Read and meditate on *Colossians 3:12-17*.

God longs for us to live in peace. Look at what Paul admonished us to be clothed with in *Colossians 3:12*. Consider these attributes as you seek to live in peace with your spouse and come to an understanding with regard to discipline.

Consider what is best for your family. What is best for your children as a whole? What is best for your marriage? Seek to find a place of compromise with your spouse regarding discipline. God desires that this be an opportunity for you to grow together, rather than be torn apart. When discussing these issues, remember this is not a competition to win or lose. It is an opportunity for the two of you to come together and make decisions based on what is best for your children and your family.

Don't try to control the parenting style of parents outside your home. As difficult as it may be for your family, you cannot control what happens with your children outside of your home. Whether you maintain joint custody with 50/50 visitation or whether your children see their non-custodial parent for visitation every other weekend, you cannot be assured of consistency in styles of discipline.

While certainly not optimal, you can make the best out of a difficult situation. Even though you cannot maintain consistency household to household, you can bring security to your children by being consistent in your own household. There may or may not be rules in the other household your child visits or resides within, but you will do your child a great service by maintaining consistent boundaries in your own home.

I know for us, there were lots of prayers offered up for the protection of two of our children while they went to visit their non-custodial parent. Know that while you cannot control, you can pray and trust God to take care of your children while they are out of your supervision. *"If possible, so far as it depends on you, be at peace with all men." Romans 12:18*

You and your spouse are a team. While it may not always feel like it, you and your spouse are on the same team. You are not opponents. But you are running toward the same goal line. Don't let disagreement sideline your family and your marriage. Try to hear the heart of your spouse when you disagree with regard to discipline. Asking questions with the goal of better understanding will help you come to an agreement somewhere in the middle.

When it comes to stepchildren, allow the biological parent to take the lead. As a step-parent you are there to help, encourage and support the biological parent. While you may not always agree with them, you need to support their decisions. Choose a time when the children are not present to calmly discuss your disagreements. The biological parent may already feel pulled between children and an ex-spouse. Be their cheerleader instead of additional opposition.

As a step-parent, you are a support for the biological parent, not a replacement. I know it may be difficult, especially if you are the stepmom, to not take over raising all the children. And being an at-home mom brings even more challenges. But it is important to remember that although you may have responsibilities to care for stepchildren, you are not a replacement parent. Most of the time, the children already have two parents. As a step-parent you can love and nurture the stepchildren. You may even have to discipline on occasion, just be sure you are in communication with your spouse and that you are both on the same page. As time passes and trust between the two of you is built, you can more freely parent even your stepchildren.

Let the biological parent take the lead in parenting. They have a history with and understanding of their own children. If the biological parent feels as though the step-parent is in opposition with respect to the children, the wedge built in the marriage becomes very difficult to remove. *"By wisdom a house is built, and by understanding it is established; and by knowledge the rooms are filled with all precious and pleasant riches." Proverbs 24:3-4*

Take a deep breath. I know this has been an intense lesson. Perhaps you need to focus on just one of the principles for now and ask God to help you understand it and live within it.

What parenting principle seems most natural to your family?

What is the most challenging principle to implement and apply in your family?

Pray for your spouse, and all the children who live in your home. Trust God with your family. Thank Him for your family.

Day Four

Communication

One of the most difficult aspects of any relationship seems to be developing positive communication habits. Being in a subsequent marriage often amplifies the difficulty. When couples in first marriages come together, they bring with them the habits and lifestyles developed in their family of origin. Relational patterns between spouses are not yet deeply ingrained, and if issues are recognized and addressed early in the relationship, positive communication patterns can be developed. As you may recall, this week's beatitude teaches the importance of being a peacemaker. Positive and healthy communication is foundational to having peace in your stepfamily.

If, however, the subsequent marriage is entered with deeply rooted communication issues from previous relationships, the chances of overcoming those unhealthy habits decrease. Subsequent marriages and blending families must be more proactive and aggressive when addressing negative communication patterns.

Let me also say, that not all the things brought to the new marriage and family are bad. Some divorced couples had good relationships. Some even continue to have good relationships. Additionally, subsequent marriages resulting from the death of a spouse are likely more positive. So just because a relationship ended, through either death or divorce, does not automatically presuppose there were major communication issues.

Even in good relationships, there is still room for improvement. No marriage is perfect. No family is perfect. We can always strive to be better. In our previous family relationship, we developed certain habits and patterns based on the people in our family. We knew them. We understood their style. We probably knew how to speak their love language and we understood their personality type. We could anticipate how they would react in most settings, and knew how to handle conflict based on the personalities in the home.

However, now, there are a different set of people, with different personalities and styles. We must [re]learn how to manage communication in this new family. So, whether there are communication issues to confront or you simply want to fine-tune communication in your already harmonious home, here are some suggestions based on God's Word.

👣 Read Ephesians 4:17-5:2.

What is the contrast Paul draws between the Gentiles and the Ephesian believers?

What does Paul tell the Ephesian church to "put on" and "take off"?

What does Paul say about anger?

What does he say about stealing?

What does Paul warn about talk?

What are we to get rid of?

What are we to do instead?

Paul gives us quite a list to follow as we relate with others. This section in my NIV is labeled "Living as Children of Light." He uses the contrast between the Gentile unbelievers and the Ephesian believers to help us understand our calling as Christ-followers.

When you are seeking to be the peacemaker in your blending home and family, these principles are critical to equip you to be the light in your home. While you are not likely leading a bunch of heathens (although sometimes it may feel like it), you are called to set an example as a child of light for those you influence. Let's break down what Paul is teaching.

First, Paul exhorts his listeners to no longer live as they did previously, when they were in the dark and carrying a hardened heart. There may have been things in your previous relationship that were difficult and heavy. You may have felt like darkness was overcoming you. Your heart may have been hardened if you were dealing with rejection or betrayal from one who once professed to love you.

But Paul gives you another alternative. He says that just like you remove a dirty garment, you are to "put off" your former way of life … your old self. While you are being made new in the attitude of your mind, you have the opportunity to put on a new garment. Jesus shared with you the truth of how to live in victory. You begin by allowing Him to transform your mind. He can give you a new perspective. He is able to redeem the attitudes you embrace that prevent you from living victoriously.

In Christ, you have the power to live in true righteousness and holiness. Christ comes into your life to transform you. He comes to make all things new. Regardless of your attitudes or hurt, your rejection or pain, Christ can transform all those difficult attitudes. He can give you a new perspective. He can restore and redeem your life and your family.

Because of Christ in you, you can begin to change your behaviors, your reactions and your relationships. Paul provides a list of examples of things that can change once we "put on" the righteousness and holiness of Christ. He says we can put off falsehood and speak truthfully to our neighbor.

He addresses anger, giving instruction for how to handle our inevitable anger with Christlikeness. He says although we will experience anger, our anger does not need to lead us to sin. How can anger lead to sin? As you know, there are a number of things that tend to trigger our anger. Those things are often uncontrollable. Yet, with the power of the Holy Spirit in us, we can control how we respond in our anger.

If you have a short fuse and tend to react now and regret it later, God gives you the opportunity to allow His Spirit in you to do the responding. You must be willing. If so, the Holy Spirit will empower you to overcome the flesh so that your anger does not cause you to sin.

Paul also gives us another important instruction with regard to anger. I think it is particularly important in families and especially in marriages. When he tells his listeners to **not** let the sun go down on their anger, he is implicating the importance of quickly resolving anger between individuals. Think about it. How many nights have you lost sleep because you are seething over something your mate did or didn't do, said or didn't say that made you angry? Regardless of your motive for silence, you kept you anger concealed (or at least you thought you did) and as the evening wore on, instead of your anger subsiding and reason taking over, your anger became deeper and louder and more irrational. What does that do to your relationship with your mate?

By the time dawn arrives, you are so angry you can barely even speak. The enemy has won the battle and has formed a wedge between you and your mate. There is discord and hurt. The enemy has a foothold in your marriage. Your response to anger has invited the enemy to come in and come between the two of you.

When handling anger, especially in your family, it is vital to deal with it quickly. While sometimes there is the necessity for a time of cooling off, there should always be a follow up with rational discussion and intentional listening between the people involved. Whether it is you and your spouse, you and your children, or you and your stepchildren, it is critically important to the health of your family that you deal with anger quickly. Here are a few suggestions inspired by Paul's teachings.

Don't let your anger dictate an immediate response. Allow yourself time to cool off before you do or say something you will regret. Many times we speak words in anger that we would give anything to take back. We tend to be irrational and selfish when our anger is ignited. Take a few minutes to cool off, pray and form rational thoughts. Sometimes, when we step back, we realize perhaps our immediate anger was not only about the situation sparking the explosion. Perhaps there were things which happened at work or during the day that had your fuse primed and ready to ignite. Perhaps the source of your anger wasn't even about the object of your anger. Your offender was just in the wrong place at the wrong time. Take time to analyze and form rational thoughts about your anger before responding.

Don't let your anger seethe. While you may need time to cool off, be intentional with your thoughts during that time. Sometimes anger likes to replay times the object of your anger has set you off. Be careful with absolutes in your thinking ... words like always and never. Allow your heart to see the person you are angry with through the filter of God's love. If it is your mate who has offended you or hurt you, remember that you love them. Even when they make you angry. Anger loves to keep score. But the truth is, when it comes to differences of opinions or perspectives, there is no winner.

Let God direct you in your anger. There is a battle for control over your anger. The enemy would love to bury you and your relationships in anger. God longs to lift you above it. Trust God with your anger and allow His word and His character to fill your mind and heart.

Paul also has some wisdom with regard to our perspective of others. While he talks about the one who steals, I think there is an application for how we live our lives. I know when I first looked at this passage, I thought this really did not apply to me. I am not a thief. Yet, while I may not lift a candy bar from the local convenience store, I have to look at the application beyond thievery. Look at how Paul follows his comment about not stealing. He says we must work, doing something useful with our own hands so that we might have something to share with those in need.

Do you work to provide for the needs of those in your family? And I am not just talking about a roof, food and clothing. People have needs beyond just the physical. What is your labor of love to help those in your family feel appreciated and included? Are you stealing from them in intangible ways? How do you respond to your stepchildren when they say or do hurtful things to you or your children? I don't want to reach beyond the message of Paul's words, but I do think he gives us opportunity to at least ponder how each of us might be stealing.

To conclude, Paul puts it bluntly. He says we are to control the things that come out of our mouth. He says to let **no** unwholesome talk be spoken. And in case there is any question about what unwholesome talk means, he provides an explanation in *Ephesians 4:31*.

Do the words you speak to your family members build them up or tear them down? Are you speaking words that are beneficial to those who hear the words, or are your words spoken just so you can vent and feel better? The total focus of Paul's instruction is on the listener, not the one who is speaking.

Evaluate what you say and how you say it. Ask yourself how your words and your tone are impacting the listener. Do your children and stepchildren feel built up after you have spoken? Does your spouse feel encouraged and respected by your words? Stop and evaluate the impact your words have on those around you.

Paul ends this discourse with some specific examples. He tells us what to get rid of, and he tells us what to replace it with. You can see the list of what to throw out. But I want to focus on what Paul says to do instead.

Be kind. Life is tough. Stress seems to be a constant companion. It does not always feel like people really care that much about how their words impact us. But Paul says to let kindness mark you. Let kindness become your default. Allow God to perform a miracle in your heart, taking out the bitterness and anger and replacing it with kindness.

Be compassionate. This word compassion is similar to empathy. If you can see others with a heart of love and understanding, you can experience compassion. When your stepchildren rail against you or speak to you unkindly, listen to what is behind their words. Try to understand their feelings. They have lost their family. They have a parent who is somewhat estranged. They are insecure because they wonder if they are in some way responsible for the dissolution of their family. They are hurting. They may be afraid and lonely. They have been thrust into a family they may or may not feel comfortable with. Try to hear their heart. Then, respond to them with compassion.

Forgive one another. While we covered a detailed understanding of forgiveness in an earlier lesson, this is a good reminder of the power forgiveness has in your life and relationships. Forgiveness is probably one of the most difficult things we do. As humans, we are wired to look for justice and fairness. We are committed to guarding our own rights and well-being. But if you are living in a family, here's an absolute truth. You will get hurt. You will be treated unfairly. Those you love will disappoint you. The question you must ask yourself is, how will you choose to respond when (not if) these things happen?

The greatest gift you can give yourself and your family is to operate with a heart of forgiveness. Let go of the need to retaliate. Let go of the need to keep account of wrongs. There may be an ex-spouse causing your family all kinds of grief. Let it go. There may be stepchildren who treat you unfairly. Let it go. Your spouse may hurt you in the way they choose to deal with their ex-spouse. Let it go. You may be hurt by the relationship between stepsiblings. Let it go. Remember, forgiveness is a choice long before it is a feeling. You must choose it before you feel it. So, for today, choose to forgive.

Paul reminds us that we are to forgive as Christ forgave. He died for you. While you were still a sinner, He was crucified for your sin. You owed a debt you could never pay. He stepped in and paid it for you. You did not deserve it. You did not earn it. You hurt Him. You rejected Him. You betrayed Him. Yet Love stepped in and He forgave you for everything you will ever do that hurts Him. That is forgiveness. Perhaps these words will help you as you choose to be a peacemaker in your home.

Enough for today. Take time to process what we have covered. Let God speak to your heart.

 Has God especially spoken to you about something we have covered today? If so, journal your thoughts.

Trust Him and allow Him to begin to transform your heart and your actions.

Day Five

Setting Boundaries

It may seem strange to include a study on setting boundaries in the midst of a week where we are focusing on being a peacemaker. But sometimes, lack of boundaries are the very thing that causes great conflict. Setting boundaries is important in any family, but can be especially important when you are bringing together two families and children from previous marriages.

While children will feel a loss of control over their life, providing a safe place with secure boundaries will begin to rebuild some of the stability and security every child longs for and needs. How can you set boundaries that are clear, fair and helpful, without feeling like the family police officer? Let's look to God's Word for some help.

All throughout scripture, God has set boundaries for His people. Even in the Garden of Eden, God placed boundaries for Adam and Eve. Throughout the history of Israel, there were boundaries set by God. He set physical land boundaries, but He also set boundaries for righteousness. He set boundaries to help us know how to live well. So why wouldn't He want us to set boundaries for our families.

Psychologists tell us that although children often rebel against the boundaries we set for them, they actually experience love and security within those boundaries. While they may push against them, one of the greatest gifts we can give our children are solid, immovable boundaries. Consider what some of the boundaries you set might include. Especially when establishing boundaries or guidelines for children, there are some important points to remember.

Make sure the boundaries you have set are reasonable and achievable. There is nothing more frustrating or defeating than being set up to fail. Be careful when setting boundaries, making sure they are reasonable and attainable. Children still need the freedom to be children. However, reasonable boundaries help them understand the importance of self-discipline. Achievable boundaries help them build confidence and encourage a healthy self-esteem. Expecting a two-year-old to make their bed every day without help is neither reasonable nor achievable. However, expecting the same of a twelve-year-old is a perfectly achievable and reasonable boundary. It is important to help equip your child for success if you have set a boundary. Help them understand exactly what you expect. You might also consider explaining why the boundary is important for *them*.

Make sure the boundaries you set are rational and do not produce stress. I don't know about you, but I have set some irrational boundaries in the heat of the moment. Sometimes anger or our own stress will tempt us to set irrational boundaries. Consider your newly-licensed sixteen-year-old has just come home 45 minutes past curfew. You have paced the floor and your mind has imagined every possible scenario ... none of them pleasant. When you hear the garage door go up your worry turns to relief which instantly ignites into anger. Your child walks through the door and the first boundary you set goes something like this: "You are grounded from driving until you are 30!" That is not a well-thought-through boundary and is both irrational and stressful. You know that you have over-reacted out of fear and anxiety. And imagine the stress and inconvenience of having to take your child everywhere they go until they turn 30. And is this even an enforceable boundary? Be sure you are calm and thinking rationally when you set boundaries.

Be sure the boundaries you set are age and ability appropriate. Again, imagine demanding that your four-year-old be responsible for washing all the dishes every evening after dinner with no assistance. Likely, it would not be long before the dishes were easy and disposable. A four-year-old on full-time dish duty would mean your breakable dishes would not last long.

Boundaries are intended for the child's success, not the parents' convenience. This can get a little sticky sometimes. We need to ask ourselves what the motive is for the boundary we have set. Let's say you have a nineteen-year-old who is back home from college for the summer. You have grown accustomed to going to bed early because it has been just you and your spouse for the last nine months. You have eighteen years' worth of sleep to catch up on. Your child is home from college and you have never been able sleep until everyone in your household is safely tucked in bed. You decide that your nineteen-year-old's curfew is 9pm each evening. Is that really an appropriate boundary for your nineteen-year-old, or is it based solely on what is most convenient for you? Consider carefully your motives for setting boundaries.

Make sure the boundaries are consistent, but dynamic. Consistency is key to effective boundaries. However, most boundaries cannot remain static. As the child grows and circumstances change, boundaries must be adapted. A good example? Bedtimes. We have all been there. Arguments over bedtime. But here is the application. The consistent boundary you set is that you will enforce bedtimes. They dynamic in this scenario is that as the child grows older, the time for bed will change. A five-year-old may need an 8:30pm bedtime. But a sixteen-year-old can handle staying up until 10pm. The consistent is we initiate a specific bedtime. The dynamic is the time changes as the child grows. We don't throw out the bedtime boundary just because we can no longer support an early hour. We maintain a bedtime, but adjust it to fit a growing child with a growing schedule.

We know boundaries are important and valuable for us to follow because God sets boundaries throughout scripture. Let's look at an example. David gives us a glimpse into some boundaries in *Psalm 16*.

🎵 *Read Psalm 16:5-11.*

Who has assigned the boundaries?

Where have the boundary lines fallen?

How does David respond to the boundaries?

What is the result of the boundaries?

What does God do in *Psalm 16:11*?

This short passage is full of encouragement for us as we seek to set boundaries for ourselves and for our families. Before we talk specifics, let's look at the general result of boundaries.

We must begin by recognizing it is God who sets the boundaries. From the Garden of Eden, to the promise of the land for Israel, to the restrictions for the heart and the actions of God's people, the boundaries are set by God Himself.

Before we can really appreciate all this means, we must remember God's nature is love. Period. *1 John 4:16* tells us that God is synonymous with love. God *is* love. Therefore, all God does is laced with His love. Discipline included. Any restrictions He may place upon His children are to protect them and give them a long and prosperous life. While we may look at God's boundaries as restrictive, we need to understand that any restriction is for our own freedom and well-being in the present and in the future.

David says it. The boundary lines God has set for him have fallen in pleasant places. The result is a delightful inheritance. When God places restrictions on our attitudes and choices, we can know they are for our very best. He knows restricting an intimate sexual relationship to marriage is most fulfilling. Therefore, He says do not commit adultery. He knows unforgiveness leads to a life of bitterness. When He tells us to forgive others as we have been forgiven, He is fully aware that true freedom and joy are experienced only when the weight of bitterness is released through forgiveness.

Trust God with the boundary lines He has set for you and trust Him to direct you as you set the boundary lines for your blending family. Notice the positive impact of the boundaries God has set. He says that our heart is glad, our tongue rejoices and our body will rest secure. These are tremendous benefits for us as individuals and for our families. Imagine the powerful impact boundaries can have on the hearts of our family as they experience joy. Imagine a life of rejoicing because of our boundaries. Imagine the rest and security available to us when we remain within the boundaries God has set!

God has a plan for you and your family and He uses the boundaries He has set to help you fulfill that plan. I love what *Psalm 16:11* says: *"You [God] have made known to me the path of life; you will fill me with joy in your presence, with eternal pleasures at your right hand."* The path of life is not a mystery. God longs to reveal the path He has already laid out for us to follow. And imagine following that path with joy and eternal pleasures because we walk alongside the Author of joy and the One who holds our eternity.

Before we move on, I want to take a minute and address David's comments in *Psalm 16:10*. This verse clearly points to the coming Messiah. David certainly found his security in the promise of the One who was to come; the One who was prophesied throughout the Old Testament; the One whom Isaiah foretold. David's confidence was found in the mere promise of the One who would come, but not be abandoned to the grave; the Holy One who's body would not see decay. Be further encouraged. We have an advantage over our brother, David, because we live on this side of the cross. We are no longer awaiting the advent of the Messiah, we now have the Messiah.

We know the Messiah. We read how He was falsely accused and crucified. We heard Him commit His Spirit into God's faithful Hand. We know His followers carried Him to the tomb of Joseph of Arimathea. We read of the women who arrive on Sunday morning with the spices to anoint the body, only to find an empty tomb and neatly folded burial garments. What David believed in His heart, we have experienced through the written Word of God. So how much more assurance do we have that God really does have this world, and our family in the palm of His Hand?

So, with this in mind, let's turn our attention toward the practical. Let's look at how we can set Godly boundaries for our family in order to experience God's direction, His joy and His eternal security.

You have people in your home who may not want to be there. You have children who once knew the security of life with biological parents and full siblings. Now these children have been torn from one of their parents and forced to accept another parent and other siblings who are not in any way biologically related to them. Setting boundaries will be critical to creating an atmosphere of harmony in your blending home. Here are a few suggestions to discuss with your spouse regarding boundaries.

Let no unwholesome talk come from your mouth. We discussed this verse earlier, but it is important that we revisit it here. Set boundaries for how your family talks to and talks about each other, and those in related family units. It almost seems natural and certainly cathartic, to be able to spew venom about the people in this new familial scenario. You, as the parents, are the ones who will set the example. It is so easy to "trash talk" the "other people." That may begin with your ex-spouse and perhaps the new mate they have chosen. There may be stepchildren who stay on your last nerve. However, God's command to you is to speak to them and about them with gentleness and compassion. While it is important for children to feel the freedom to share their thoughts and feelings, it is equally important to teach them how to view others as Jesus does. While you may need to listen to them "throw up" about your new mate or a stepsibling, it is important, after valuing their feelings, to help reframe their perspective. Help them find positive things or ways they might connect with those they are struggling with the most.

Love your neighbor as yourself. Remember when the religious leaders were trying to trap Jesus with a verbal shell game? They were trying to talk Him into a corner about which was the greatest commandment. What they failed to recognize is that the Author of those commandments was standing right in front of them, and certainly understood the underlying principles behind the rules that had been laid down for the children of Israel. Jesus tried to help them understand that the rules God set were simply an example for what He wanted from the heart of His people. Jesus answered their question by stating the first and greatest commandment was to love the Lord with all their heart, soul and mind. If you look at the Ten Commandments that deal with man's relationship with God, you see this very concept behind each of the "rules." He went on to say that, although they didn't ask, there was a second great commandment which was like the first one. But it dealt with others. Look at the Ten Commandments that deal with man's relationships with man. Do you see it? Jesus told them they were to love their neighbor as they love themselves. Does your blending family love each other well? Are they so busy trying to protect their turf and their stuff they forget about the value each person in the household brings? You and your spouse will have your hands full modeling this, but it is critical for your children to see you loving each other and loving them well. While no family can achieve perfection, we can all strive to value, encourage and have compassion for every member of the family.

When our children were younger and at home, we were always trying to come up with creative ideas to help encourage them to value the true meaning of Christmas. One year, we decided to help them understand that Christ came in love, to give all He had, even His life so that everyone could have an eternity spent with Him in heaven. A part of this object lesson had to do with modeling the heart of Christ by how we treated each other. So, we decided to take the month of December to make a bed for the baby Jesus. We talked about the importance of providing a warm, soft place for a baby to sleep. We talked about how Mary and Joseph used hay to make a soft, warm place for baby Jesus to lay His Head. Then, we took a manger (probably an extra laundry basket if memory serves) and put it under the tree. Next to it was another basket filled with yellow strips of construction paper. The assignment was to make a soft bed for Jesus. The way that happened was, when someone in our family did something nice for another, the recipient of the kindness then got to add some "hay" to the manger. By Christmas morning, we would see how soft the bed where we put baby Jesus had become. How much kindness did our family provide to make a soft bed for the baby? While there may have actually been some "hay" bargaining that went on between siblings, it at least made everyone more aware of how they treated each other. And I think there was actually some relational mending that took place.

Everyone is allowed personal space. While this is not really a biblical principle, we learned the hard way that it is really important to children (and parents), especially early in the family's life to feel a sense of ownership of what is "theirs." You may have children who have to share rooms. Your house may suddenly seem small and crowded after trying to combine things from two households. You may have to get creative, but try as much as possible to give everyone at least a corner somewhere that they can call their own, where they can retreat when they need to have some space. That space may be defined by including some items that are important to each child. While sharing is so important, there are just a few things that may not need to be shared. Each of our children had a thing or two that had been their security through difficult days and painful transitions. We allowed those few items to be "off limits" to the other children in our family. I was honestly amazed at the level of respect each of the children had for the items of others. And allow children to set boundaries of "alone time" (within reason) when they need it. It is important to, again, model for children the importance of time alone for refilling without requiring constant aloneness.

As parents, we need alone time as well. We learned early on that it was important to set our own boundaries. It is perfectly acceptable to tell your children you need to be alone. However, it is also important you tell them how long before you are available, and even more important to stick with the time you have told them. Make sure they know you are not angry or upset, but you just need a few minutes of solitude. Then take the time to be alone. Once you are refreshed, they will find you to be a much more relaxed, engaged parent.

Finally, as a couple, parents need the opportunity to be alone. You may be able to go out on a date by yourselves once a week. If not, you need to carve out some time when the kids understand you are not to be disturbed. When all of our kids were home, we would occasionally take an evening for ourselves. We had a baby and four older children. We would put the baby to bed, and let one of the older kids take turns with the baby monitor. I think the kids enjoyed it too, because we would usually let them have dinner in the family room in front of a movie. Then, we would have a picnic in our bedroom floor and usually watch a movie together. Then, after the movie, we would retrieve the baby monitor and tuck the kids in bed. When your children see you value your relationship as a couple, they are learning how to have a healthy marriage of their own someday.

While this is hardly an exhaustive list of possible boundaries, perhaps it will get you started. The bottom line with boundaries has to do with respect. We need to respect ourselves and our own need for solitude, but we also need to respect others and their need to have time alone. Respecting other's space and property will go a long way in establishing a safe, secure and happy home.

🐾 As we close the study for today, consider how setting boundaries can provide a peaceful home. As a peacemaker, what boundaries can you set to help keep the peace in your family?

What are some boundaries unique to your stepfamily's situation?

What are some challenges your stepfamily faces regarding boundaries?

Spend some time in prayer asking God to direct you as you set boundaries for your family. What is God speaking to you about being a peacemaker? Has He prompted you to consider a boundary or two in your home that will help instill a peaceful atmosphere? Thank God for a peace that passes all understanding. Trust Him to help you be the peacemaker.

> *"You're blessed when you can show people how to cooperate instead of compete or fight. That's when you discover who you really are, and your place in God's family." Matthew 5:9 (The Message)*

Week Eight

When Bad Things Happen to Good People

"Blessed are those who are persecuted because of righteousness, for theirs is the kingdom of heaven." Matthew 5:10

Have you ever wondered why things happen as they do? Have you ever felt like no matter what you had done or not done, you were paying consequences you did not earn? There are times in our lives when things simply do not make sense. We try to do things God's way, yet it seems as though we are penalized for our righteousness. The further along I go through life, the less and less surprised I am by things. What once seemed to be justice, now leaves me standing, awestruck, wondering where the justice has gone.

People who are truly seeking righteousness seem to be the very ones who are condemned. The person who remains in sin seems to have everything go their way. In the world of blending families, we hear so many stories of how people came to be in their new blending family. As I hear stories of divorce and abandonment, I cease to be shocked at what people go through. Courts rule in favor of adulterous spouses. Money changes hands based on anything but what is right by moral standards.

As we begin this week's study, I hope you will be able to go to God with an open and willing heart. You may have been the one who felt persecuted at the hand of someone who was not living righteously. You may have felt unfairly judged. It may be that in your view, you did not get a fair shake. Hopefully the lessons this week will help you reframe your circumstances and gain a new perspective.

I don't know where you are on your journey as a blending family. I don't know if there are still issues you encounter with an ex-spouse. I don't know if you have problems with adult stepchildren. But wherever you are, you can find opportunities to grow. This week we are considering being persecuted for righteousness. As the lessons unfold, I challenge you to look at each time when you feel as though you have been unfairly treated, but have not been in the wrong, as an opportunity to allow God to teach you and mold you. Allow Him to help you see your situation through His eyes, and trust Him to take care of you and your family.

As we end our study this week, we will consider this final beatitude. But I also want to provide a few days of practical suggestions. I hope you will find opportunities to see what

God is doing in you and in your family. I hope you have learned some things that have helped you personally, in your marriage, and in your family.

Remember, it is never too late to start fresh. While there may be mistakes in your blending family, and regrets you have over some things you have allowed in your blending family, I hope you will view today as a fresh start for you and your family. You may be doing things well, and have a very successful family. But there are always areas for growth. Allow God to show you areas where He desires to strengthen your family. Realize, however, that no person or family is ever perfect. Let go of the things you can't change. Resolve to change the things you can. Trust God with your tomorrows.

As you step into the lesson this week, spend some time with God, and prepare your heart to hear His message for you today.

A Lesson from Job

Perhaps one of the most difficult stories in the Bible tells the story of a righteous man named Job. I remember being afraid to read this book of the Bible. I thought if I learned about Job, God might one day ask me to live his life. It is a sometimes frightening tale that chronicles the life of one of God's most faithful.

Before we jump into the study, let's get a little bit of background. Job was probably one of the greatest examples of someone who was persecuted for their righteousness. Only it wasn't martyrdom like we usually think. In fact, I am often deeply troubled by the stories of some of the early church martyrs. When I was studying for my Master's degree in Theology, one of the required courses was Christian History. I had an amazing professor who knew more stories than I could imagine. I loved the class because he always told the "behind the scenes" kind of stories; things that were so interesting and made the events we studied so real. As he regaled us with story after story of what happened to early Christians, I would sometimes have to fight back tears. People whose lives were taken simply because of their faith in Christ. They were tortured and suffered horrific deaths at the hands of evil.

But Job is a little bit different. While he experienced profound loss, it really was not directly at the hands of other people. His losses were perpetrated straight from the pit of hell.

🕮 *Read Job 1:1-5.*

Record everything you learn about Job.

I think we could sum up Job's life by saying he was a righteous man who desired to please God. He even sacrificed on behalf of his grown children just in case they had sinned. He was well respected and by all accounts lived his life honoring God and receiving God's favor.

🕮 *Read Job 1:6-12.*

Whose idea was it for Satan to "touch" Job's life?

As you read this passage, perhaps your response is like mine. God goes to Satan and draws Job to his attention. God describes Job as a man who is blameless and upright, who fears God and shuns evil. While I have often heard this story told, the storyteller sometimes misses this part. I have often heard it said that Satan went to God and asked for Job, and God relented. I think when we consider a loving God and His righteous follower, we have a hard time understanding the way this exchange actually happened. There is no doubt God singles Job out. God, Himself launched the initiative for trials to come upon Job. Trials that would blindside Job and potentially push him into failure. Of course, Satan was delighted to unleash his evil on Job.

We just have a hard time grasping why God would basically give Satan the idea to torment Job. Job was a righteous man. He was upright and God-fearing. Yet, God actually asked Satan to consider Job.

🐾 What did Satan say to God in *Job 1:9*?

Satan felt like Job's righteousness was tied to God's favor. Remove God's favor and Job would crumble and curse God. I can only imagine what Satan was thinking just now. He thought he had painted God into a corner and Job would crash and burn at the hand of the enemy's torment.

But God never gets painted into a corner. He is always in control of every situation. If we believe what we say, that God knows us better than we know ourselves, He knew exactly how Job would respond when Satan's fury was unleashed. So God allowed Satan to do his evil work in the life of Job. One very important point in this story. God is sovereign. Satan could not do anything to Job that God did not allow. He could only touch Job's life to the point that God permitted. Satan can never overstep the boundaries God has placed upon him.

This is important to remember any time we are suffering. God is always in control. Satan does not have any authority or activity in our life outside of what God allows.

🐾 *Read Job 1:13-19.*

What did Satan take from Job?

Can you imagine being Job? In the span of a few brief moments, he learns that he has lost his livestock which was his livelihood and all his source of income, his source of transportation and all of his children. Each calamity was interrupted by another, worse calamity. Have you ever had a day or season like that? You are afraid to utter the words,

167

"what else could happen?" As soon as you do, something else does happen. It can't get any worse, but it does. You can't bear one more thing, but one more thing happens.

🕮 *Read Job 1:20-22.*

What was Job's response to the news?

As I read Job's response, I find the first three things he did completely understandable. He got up, tore his robe and shaved his head. This was how he expressed mourning over the catastrophic losses he had just suffered. But the next thing he did is baffling. He had just lost almost everything he had, but in the midst of his mourning and grief, he chose to worship God.

🕮 Record what Job says in *Job 1:21*.

I am always amazed as I read these words. In the midst of life's deepest loss, Job focuses on God and ends his discourse in praise. He recognizes God as the giver of all things and that God also has the right to take away anything He chooses. Instead of questions of why me, and bitterness, Job responds in praise.

🕮 Write out *Job 1:22*.

This is an incredible story. Even when Job was losing everything he held dear, he was able to trust God and even praise him. In the midst of financial ruin, he was able to look to God without question, but with a voice of praise.

The challenge for me as I read this account, is to ponder how I have responded in the face of loss. While I have had some very painful days along life's journey, I must admit I have never experienced a day like Job's. I have to look at how I respond when things seem unfair. What is the state of my heart when someone takes something precious from me? How do I respond when God allows me to experience loss? Do I stomp my feet and scream at God that this is not fair? Do I retaliate and wish the worst on the offender?

What about you? When adversity comes, how do you respond? Do you trust God no matter what? Are you able to recognize God's sovereignty and have faith that His ways are the best ways? I often think of a Babbie Mason song from the 1980's. It's called *Trust His Heart*. Part of the chorus says:

> *"God is too wise to be mistaken, God is too good to be unkind,*
> *When you can't see His plan, when you don't understand,*
> *When you can't trace His Hand, trust His heart."*[6]

🙏 How you respond in the face of adversity reveals what you believe about God. Do you really believe He loves you, cares for you, and has your best interest at heart?

If so, do you trust Him with what happens in your life?

I hope today's lesson has given you some things to consider. While we won't study all of Job's experiences, we will spend a little more time with him tomorrow to see what happens in the rest of the story.

🙏 What has God spoken to you today?

How is He prompting you to respond to what you have learned?

How do you typically handle loss?

When it comes to grief, what is your most natural response?

Spend some time in prayer, listening to Him and responding as He has called you.

Day Two

Our friend Job ... There's More ...

Yesterday we left Job in the midst of loss. His livelihood was gone. His children were all gone. He was left in the midst of his grief to sort out what had happened. As onlookers, we are still baffled at why God would allow such calamity in the life of a righteous, upstanding man. We may still be trying to rationalize why God would send Satan to torment this Godly man. But his story is far from over.

Read Job 2:1-10.

What else does God allow Satan to do to Job?

What does Job's wife have to say?

How does Job reply?

I can only imagine what Job's life was like after losing everything. I would imagine that with each passing day, he sought to rebuild his life. He may have even felt some relief, believing the worst had come and gone, and surely there would be no more suffering. Then, Satan and God had another conversation. God was not finished with Job. God recounts Job's response to his losses. Next, Satan is allowed to afflict Job with a physical malady. And a miserable one at that. It reminds me of when my first husband was going through his first round of chemotherapy to fight his cancer. The treatments were very aggressive and required that he remain in the hospital. During his second week of treatments, he began to develop the more severe side-effects of a three chemo-drug cocktail. He formed sores in his mouth that apparently went all the way down his esophagus. He developed a rash all over his body that itched terribly, but was also incredibly painful to touch. Misery inside and out. He required around-the-clock intravenous drugs to combat the side-effects. I often thought about Job as I watched him suffer. How awful it must have been for Job. But

170

even in the midst of the most awful physical suffering, he still chose to remain upright and righteous. Job continued to honor God in his suffering.

Enter Job's friends. While we won't read the chapters that outline the conversation between Job and his friends, we will discuss the contents. When they first came to Job, they were so upset by what they saw and the great suffering of their friend, that for seven days and seven nights they sat in silence and just hurt alongside their friend.

I want to stop the story here and give you a word about ministry to those who are hurting. Although later in the story we will see the damage words can do, Job's friends did well initially by their silence. When someone is suffering, often times, the best thing we can do is just be with them. Words don't help them feel any better. At the risk of sounding sacrilegious, this is not the best time to begin spouting every Bible verse you have ever learned. In the church world, we call this the ministry of presence. When someone is hurting, usually what they need the most is just have someone to be with them. No words. No answers. No suggestions. Not even encouragement. Just be with them. Honestly, Job's friends got it right. Until they opened their mouths.

As we fast-forward the story, we find Job finally speaking. He begins to question the day of his birth. In our interpretation, he wished he had never been born. While he did not ask to die, he did wonder why he had to be born in the first place. This opened the door to his friends. They began to question and analyze and accuse. In a word, the persecution for Job had begun. Instead of encouragement, Job's friends brought words of judgment and condemnation. Instead of helping him endure, they added insult to injury. As the discussion continues, Job gets to the place where he begins to question God. His friends help lead him to a place where he does question why.

God listens to the banter before He steps in and begins to speak to Job. *Job 38:1-3* records *"Then the Lord answered Job out of the storm. He said: 'Who is this that darkens my counsel with words without knowledge? Brace yourself like a man; I will question you, and you shall answer me.'"*

Job is challenged by God's sovereignty. God helps Job understand that His ways cannot be explained or understood by mortal man. The next four chapters are spent admonishing Job. The result of Job's encounter with God is repentance. He allows God's words to penetrate his heart and give him a new perspective.

🐾 *Read Job 42.*

This story ends well for Job. But there are a few important points for us to take away from our encounter with Job and his friends.

A genuine encounter with God leads to repentance. When God spoke to Job, his heart was opened to God's truth. When we encounter God, we realize our profound need for Him. When Job encountered God, he was led to a place of repentance. While we sometimes use the words forgive and repent in the same breath, we need to understand their distinction.

Forgiveness is what God does in response to our sin. We may ask for it, God administers it. Repentance is an action on our part. Repentance literally means "to turn." That means when we are walking in sin (the wrong way), true repentance occurs when we turn away from the sin and begin to walk back toward God and righteous living. That's what God's word did for Job.

Praying for others has a positive impact upon us. When you pray for others, God brings blessings to you. Look at the order of what happened next in the story. God chastised Job's friends. He then told Job to pray for them. Job did not wait until he was healed to begin to pray. *Job 42:10* says after Job prayed for his friends, the Lord made him prosperous again. While Job had no idea that God would restore anything to him, he was still obedient to pray for his friends. The result of his obedience? God blessed him greatly.

Pray for those who persecute you. This story gives us insight on praying for our persecutors. Few of us will likely find ourselves in the midst of true persecution. But we all will encounter times when we are criticized for our faith. We may even lose jobs or relationships when we stand up for our faith. However, Job teaches us that no matter what happens, we must pray for our persecutors.

God is faithful. It is important to point out that God will not always give you a *Job 42* ending to your story of persecution. Many people have lost lives, family, and livelihood because of their faith. Not everyone gets to have their lives restored after persecution. Yet, we do know that God is faithful. We can trust Him in the midst of our persecution.

In the midst of your life and family, you may encounter persecution. Trust God when it happens. Allow Him to teach you and encourage you as you remain faithful to Him. We live in a world that is hostile to God and His ways. You can expect to experience some form of persecution as you journey. Let Job be a source of hope. He showed us so much about trusting God in the face of persecution. Know the enemy is always at the root. He uses people and events to persecute, but remember it is God's sovereignty that is controlling the activity of the enemy.

🐾 Do you recall a time when you felt personally attacked for doing the right thing, or standing up for your faith? Describe your experience.

How did you respond?

If you had it to do all over again, what would you do differently?

Spend some time in prayer reflecting on what God is teaching you. This may have been a challenging lesson for you today. Thank you for your perseverance!

Day Three

So what about Job?

I hope you were able to gain some insight and encouragement from Job as we consider being persecuted for righteousness. But, you may be wondering what all this has to do with blending your family. I want to be careful about making correlations here, but I think we could all agree that there have been times when things in your blending family have felt unfair. You are doing your best to live righteously, yet it seems as though you are taking the wrath of others in your household. It is vital to remember that while every story has two sides, there are also times when things seem wrongly weighted. You feel unjustly accused of something. There are people who treat you disrespectfully for no apparent reason. There is anger and frustration pointed your way, and you are honestly not sure why.

Part of this is just life. People have different perspectives, and while you may feel like you are the "righteous" one, there may be others who do not share your perspective. Even if you are still in the midst of dealing with an ex-spouse and issues that continue to arise, it may be difficult to see things objectively. But even if you are the one who is being treated unfairly, please consider the bottom line desire of God's heart. Regardless of who is "righteous" and who is not, God longs for restored relationships as much as possible. We have discussed this in previous lessons, but this is a good opportunity for another helpful reminder.

Job obviously had to release some of his feelings about his friends when he prayed for them. There is power in forgiveness and moving on. Whether it's your ex-spouse or a stepchild, if you have any ill feelings, take it to God in prayer. It is through prayer God can most effectively change your heart. Take some time to consider these principles we learned from Job.

Sometimes life does not seem fair. Job did not do anything to deserve what he got. In fact, he was doing everything right. Even according to God. Yet, bad things happened to him that were completely out of his control. Not only did he suffer personally, but his friends even began to cast judgment against poor Job. You may feel as though your friends abandon you when things are really the worst. You may feel condemned and judged when you are in the midst of your hurt. You may have lost some friends as your family began blending. There may have been those who "took sides" when your previous marriage ended. You can't change what people think. You can only let it go, and trust God to restore your confidence and trust in others.

In a blending family, we are often tempted to compare stories, children and the circumstances that brought the family together. Consider what you can do to help prevent the comparison game. Record your thoughts, and find a time when you and your spouse can discuss your thoughts.

Be careful about judging others who are encountering tragedy. It is so easy to look for reasons why tragedy strikes. I don't know if it is our need for understanding or simply our fear that does it, but when something tragic happens to someone we seem to have a great need to understand why. As I have considered the responses I received when my first husband became ill, I began to recognize people found personal comfort in understanding why. If they could figure out why this was happening in my family, then they could prevent it in their own. But as we see with Job, there was nothing he could have done to change what happened to him.

Job was judged by his friends. Perhaps you felt, or continue to feel, judged by others for your divorce or [re]marriage. God led Job to handle the judgment by praying for his friends.

🐾 Write down the names or initials of those who have brought you pain through judgment. Spend time praying for them.

Develop a strong spiritual connection with God during the easy times. Job was able to endure the difficulties in his life because he already had a strong spiritual foundation. Don't wait until difficulties come to develop a consistent prayer life. Spend consistent time in the Word all the time … good times and bad. Allow God to strengthen you and fill you up when life is easier.

How can you be spiritually prepared when difficulty comes? If we follow the life of Jesus and how he handled adversity, we find His lifestyle was one of spiritual discipline. He knew God's Word. He spent time in prayer. He found strength in His community of faith, both formally and informally. By that I mean Jesus was consistent to worship on the Sabbath and gather with other believers. He also surrounded Himself with a group of believers who could encourage Him along the way. As you develop a lifestyle of spiritual discipline, you will find empowering by doing what He did.

Spend time regularly studying and applying God's Word to your life. God can equip you for all things through His Word. You must know it to apply it. The only way to learn it is to spend time reading and seeking to understand how to apply God's Word to your life.

Spend time in prayer. Paul exhorts us to pray without ceasing (*1 Thessalonians 5:17*). Paul is not telling us to do nothing but pray, what he is saying is we are to pray while we do everything. Prayer is two-fold. As with Jesus, we need times where we get away to spend time alone with God. But we are also to live in an attitude of communicating with God as we go about life.

Regularly gather for worship with other believers. We are in the world most of the week. The world is a difficult place. God understands we garner strength from gathering together. We can encourage one another. We can pray for one another. We are empowered as we worship God corporately. *"And let us consider how we may spur one another on toward love and good deeds, not giving up meeting together, as some are in the habit of doing, but encouraging one another—and all the more as you see the Day approaching"* Hebrews 10:24-25. We are reminded of the importance of gathering regularly for worship with other believers.

Be a part of a small group of believers. We are created to live life in community. After creation was complete and God had pronounced that everything was good, He declared there was one thing that was not good. He said it was not good for man to be alone (*Genesis 2:18*). While God was referring to man's need for a mate, He also points to our need for others. As Jesus ministered, He had a community of faith, but He also surrounded Himself with a smaller community of close friends. We all need to surround ourselves with a small, trusted group of Christ-followers to encourage our journey.

Don't let the hard times catch you spiritually empty. God desires to speak to you all the time. It is much easier to hear Him in the darkness when you are accustomed to the clarity of His voice in the light.

🐾 What could you do to develop a deeper spiritual discipline in one of these areas?

Trust God's heart despite how circumstances appear. Job trusted God. He did not just trust God's activity in his life. Job trusted God. There will be times in life when we do not understand our circumstances. But if we consistently trust God, we will be able to endure, even if our "why" is never answered. God loves you and He has a plan for your life. No matter how things appear to be, you can trust God's Word. I know we looked at this verse earlier, but it provides a good reminder here as well. *"And we know that in all things God works for the good of those who love him, who have been called according to his purpose."* Romans 8:28.

🔖 Think of a time when you struggled to trust God in a difficult circumstance. What did you learn today that might have helped you overcome your doubt?

Spend some time with your spouse talking about these lessons from the life of Job. Pray together about anything God lays on your heart. Is there a principle God is particularly impressing upon you? Discuss how you can apply that principle in your marriage and family.

Day Four

What about the Past?

This study is coming to a close, so I would like to spend the last two days pulling together everything we have learned in order to apply it to present today. As I have pondered and prayed about how to summarize all we have learned over these weeks, I think the best ending is to evaluate how each of us deal with our past.

I know we have talked about circumstances and choices that have brought each of us to where we are today. As we have journeyed, we have collected many things along the way. Some of those things are great … things that are valuable and worth keeping. Other things are simply dead weight. Some of what we continue to carry are things that really need to be discarded. They are just slowing us down as we move forward.

When your new family came together, everyone brought suitcases with them. Even though many things in those bags were necessary and an important part of life, there were other things tucked away inside the bags that were not so essential. Some things might have been hidden amongst the underwear and toothbrushes. As life progresses, we all accumulate more things. While we have all passed through the hurt of a broken relationship, some of the things we have packed are not only needless, but can also be damaging to our new family relationships. As we move on, it becomes easy to just keep dragging the steamer trunks full of baggage with us everywhere we go. But I think God wants us to handle our past differently. When I think of the word "baggage," I am taken back to a moment in my past. Maybe you can relate.

Early in our blending days, we were extremely focused on our children and the pain they had all four suffered in their journey toward our family. My two young boys had watched their Dad die a slow and painful death. They were certainly scarred by the events of the two years leading them to his death. And they had lost one of the two most important people in their young lives. My husband's two daughters, the oldest in particular, had watched her parents' marriage dissolve into divorce. His youngest was 5-months old when the separation began, and she missed some important bonding with her biological mother. In our attempt to compensate for what they had all four endured, we tried everything we could to make their lives hence forward, idyllic.

One such attempt involved taking the kids snow skiing. We had actually planned to go over our first Christmas as a family. You know how difficult it is to manage family traditions, so we thought we would do something completely different than anything we had ever done over the holidays. So we made reservations at a great condo on Lake Keystone and booked our flights. We had purchased all the paraphernalia necessary for 10 days in the snowy mountains of Colorado. We were set. And then … chickenpox. Our oldest daughter brought them home from school just before the Christmas break. And being an experienced Mom, I did the math and determined that our youngest daughter, the only child in the house who had **not** had chickenpox would likely break out on Christmas Eve. We knew she could not fly with an infectious disease, so we begged our travel agent to change our trip to a week in January. As sure as the sun rises, our second case of chickenpox erupted during our Christmas Eve celebration.

But I digress … the baggage. So January came and we prepared to leave for our trip. There were six of us and we all had packed bulky ski clothes for the trip. Of course, each of the kids had a backpack full of things to entertain themselves on the plane. But the parents were in charge of all the checked luggage. And boy was there some checked luggage. Thankfully, this was before the days where bags had to pay to fly since we were checking ten bags. You read correctly. Ten Bags. When we landed in Denver, we realized that in order to get to the location of our pre-arranged van, we had to ride a tram. That meant getting four children, two adults, 6 backpacks and 10 pieces of luggage inside the tram door before it closed.

I will stop the story there … although I could go on and on … it was quite a trip. But what is relevant about this story pertains to the luggage. By the time we finally got to our condo, we were exhausted, stressed and frustrated, because of all the bags. We could barely even fit into the van because of all the stuff. We had sprinted our way through the airport yelling at the kids to stay close as our hands and arms were filled with stuff. I feel sure we took out a couple of people along the way.

As I reflected on the trip, I realized how much more fun we could have had while traveling if we could only have taken fewer bags. After we arrived, I wondered what we could have left at home. Honestly, I was even a bit distracted while on the trip because I was already anticipating the stress of getting all that stuff back on the plane and back home.

When it comes to our families, I think we sometimes have the same experience. When we come into a family for a second or third time, we tend to just pack all the "stuff" from our previous family and bring it along. Here is the challenge. It may be time for you to clean out some bags.

Are there bags you continue to carry that have been there so long you cannot remember what they contain? If so, spend some time opening those bags and evaluating the contents. Is there trash needing to be thrown out? You might want to write those things on a separate piece of paper. When you are ready, tear up the paper and throw it away. Allow this to stand as a reminder whenever you are tempted to revisit the "trash."

What are some issues you carry that have not been resolved? Record them. Beside the issue, write down one thing you can do to help bring resolution.

I learned during that ski trip, although we needed the big, bulky winter attire, there were things I had packed we did not even use. Over the years I have learned to pack smarter. I have traveled a lot over the past years, and the first thing I have learned is that less is more. The writer of Hebrews also has a word of encouragement about what we carry with us.

Read Hebrews 12:1-2.

What are we to "throw off"?

How are we to run?

The author of Hebrews begins by reminding us we are not alone in the race we have been called to run. There is a "cloud of witnesses" surrounding us. I envision the grandstands filled with believers who have gone on before us. Most theologians link the cloud of witnesses with those in the hall of faith, listed in *Hebrews 11*. Some think perhaps God allows our families who are already with Him to view our journey and cheer us on. But whoever is in the grandstands, they are watching us, cheering us on, and encouraging us to persevere as we run our own life's race.

The analogy of a race is important. Think about what it takes for a runner to successfully complete a race. It is impossible to successfully run a race while carrying luggage. As runners of the race, we are to throw off everything that hinders us.

What is it in your life that is hindering a successful race?

You may be carrying a heavy load as you try to run. Who are you carrying because you have not forgiven?

Is there guilt and shame you are carrying from past mistakes? Journal about those things and pray, asking God to help you let them go.

What are the hurts and pain of others in your life you are trying to carry?

It may be time to let go of the things you can't change. It may be time to stop and clean out the bags containing things not helping you succeed in the race. It may be time to let go of the guilt and pain of the past. It may be time to forgive so you can finally release the one who slows you down.

Then, there is the sin that so easily entangles. I remember a Disney movie where the enchanted castle became cursed. The princess was trapped inside and her Prince Charming was on a mission to save her. But when he and his horse rode into the castle gardens, the vines suddenly came to life and began to wrap around the hooves of the horse. After bringing the horse down, the vines continued to trap the Prince until he was tied to the ground, no longer able to move. That is the picture I have in my mind whenever I read this passage. Sin may look like a beautiful garden. But once we step into the garden, the vines suddenly begin to overtake us. We may feel powerless to stop them as they begin to slow us down. Before we know it, we are so entwined with the sin, that we are overtaken. We are no longer able to even move, much less run the race.

Be aware that sin will stop you in your tracks if you don't deal with it. God has laid out an amazing race for you to run. Satan wants nothing more than to stop you in your tracks. He wants to take everything from you. He wants to rob you of joy. He wants to keep you defeated. He wants you to be bound. But remember, *"Greater is He that is in me, than he that is in the world."* Through Christ and the power of the Holy Spirit, you are empowered to defeat the enemy and the sin that so easily entangles. There is another great truth in this passage.

𝄞 *Read Hebrews 12:2.*

The key to successfully running the race set before us is found in the very beginning of this verse. We are to *"fix our eyes on Jesus."* This does not mean we merely look with our physical eyes. We are encouraged to keep our spiritual eyes upon Jesus, the only One who can save. We are to lock our gaze upon Him so we are not distracted by anything that would take our eyes away from Him.

We see a great example of this from our friend, the apostle Peter. When He realized it was Jesus walking on the water, toward their boat, Peter wanted to step out onto the water. As long as he kept his gaze fixed on Jesus, Peter was able to do the impossible. He was able to walk on the water. But as soon as he became distracted by the circumstances around him, the waves lapping at his ankles, he began to sink.

When we keep our eyes fixed on Jesus, we can stay the course. In fact, we can even do the impossible. But we must keep our total and complete focus on Jesus and His power at work in us. After all, He is the One who authored the faith we live, and He is also the One who is perfecting it.

🐾 What does it mean to you to fix your gaze on Jesus?

What can you do today to fix your gaze on Jesus?

Your blending family is a part of the race God has set before you. If it were going to be easy, there would be no need for the admonition to persevere. There would be no need to keep our eyes fixed on Jesus. But, running a successful race is impossible unless we keep our sights set on Christ and His provision for the race.

Be willing to let go of the past as a hindrance. If there are lessons from the past God has taught you, embrace those and bring them with you. But, if you are bringing bags and bags of useless, unnecessary stuff that will just weigh you down, let it go. Throw it off. And the sin. Let it go. Give it to God. Ask forgiveness and believe that God grants it. Perhaps you need to ask Him to help you forgive yourself.

Repentance is a powerful word when trying to overcome the past. Understand that repentance is different from forgiveness. Forgiveness is what God does for you and through you. But repentance is a choice you make to turn away from the sin that entangles your journey. Repentance means to turn the other direction. It is a complete about-face. You choose to turn from sin, and walk toward the holiness God wants to grow in your life. I hope today's lesson has encouraged you to look at the baggage you have brought with you into your family.

🐾 What are some things God is asking you to let go of? Spend some time talking to God about those things.

Trust Him with the hindrances to the freedom He longs for your family to enjoy. Be honest about any sin you have brought with you. Trust Him. Close your time in prayer.

Day Five

A Time to Rejoice!

As we come to the last day of our time together, I want to leave you with a joyful heart. Probably one of the main things we would change about how we have lived over the past 18 years, is that we would have laughed more often. There were so many times when laughter would have made all the difference. But beyond laughter, there is the depth of joy that is independent of circumstances. That is where I want us to end.

I encourage you to read each of these scriptures about joy, and record what you learn from them. Then, spend some time with your spouse or even your children brainstorming ways where you can infuse more joy into your family. It is so easy to become distracted with the difficulties and negatives of a blending family. There are many opportunities tempting you to remain discouraged and stressed. But joy is a miraculous gift of the Spirit. When we have Christ in us, we already have joy residing within us. So, you can decide. How will you allow your family to affect you? Will you let it constantly be a source of stress and frustration, or will you choose joy? It is up to you. I encourage you. Choose joy.

Read Deuteronomy 16:13-15.

Record what you learn about joy.

The Feast of Tabernacles, also called the Feast of Booths, was a Jewish celebration commemorating the harvest. This is a thanksgiving celebration of God's provision for the people. It also commemorates the time in the wilderness, after God had delivered the Israelites from the hands of their Egyptian oppressors. During the wilderness wandering, the people lived in tents and even worshipped in a tabernacle, or temporary place of worship.

During this celebration the people built temporary shelters, or booths to remember that God took care of them even when they were nomads and had no permanent home. This particular feast is marked by rejoicing and celebrating for what God did for His people.

What can you do as a family to celebrate the Feast of Tabernacles? While you probably don't celebrate the Jewish holidays, you can use them as an example for choosing joy. Gather as a family and list the things God has done. Give everyone a chance to share. You might even want to write down what you remember and place it where you can see it as a reminder. Be an example by letting your family see you choose joy and express gratitude for what God is doing. Be aware this week of how you respond to things in your family. Allow God to bring joy to the surface of your attitudes and responses.

𓆡 *Read Nehemiah 8.*

This story is connected to what we learned about the Feast of Tabernacles or Booths. As you read the story, you will see that the people were grieved because, as the Book of the Law was read and explained, they saw they had not been keeping the law as they should. Midway through the story, *Nehemiah 8:10* says, *"Do not grieve, for the joy of the Lord is your strength."*

Your family may have areas where you are grieving. There may be things that surface from previous family issues. There may still be unresolved pain in the lives of the children. But in the midst of the grieving, we learn that joy in the Lord is what will give us strength to endure and overcome.

Consider that joy in the Lord is the source of your strength, and the strength of your family. God never intended for the lives of His children to be burdensome. He longs to give us all we need to live in freedom. Let joy be your default when encountering difficulties in your family.

𓆡 *Read John 15:9-11.*

Jesus reminds us that our relationship with Him is founded and built on love. He exhorts us to remain in His love. Obeying the commands of God will keep us in His love. Be careful that you don't interpret this to mean obeying God will earn His love. We can't earn God's love. He loves us because of Who He is, not because of who we are. What Jesus is trying to help us understand is that God's commands are based on His love for us. If we follow those commands, we will experience everything His love desires. Jesus goes on to say, remaining in God's love by following His commands ushers in the fullness of His joy. Imagine living a life filled with the joy of Christ! That, my friend, is an abundant life.

Commit to live out the commands of Christ in your life and family. In so doing, you are inviting the joy of Christ to envelop you and your family. The true strength of a family comes from the joy of the Lord. Do you want a strong family? Then follow Christ's commands, live in His love and invite His joy.

Remember, we began this week talking about persecution in the form of trials we experience as a blending family. Most of us will never experience persecution to the point of physical torture. However, *Matthew 5:10* tells us that the choice to live a righteous life is not always easy, but is profoundly rewarding. The same is true with your [re]marriage and stepfamily. Choosing righteousness as a family is a real challenge. But be encouraged. Righteousness is also rewarding. Choosing to live rightly by letting go of unnecessary baggage, deciding to forgive, fixing your eyes on Jesus, and allowing joy to fill your home results in a strong marriage, a healthy family, and a renewed you.

The questions I want to leave with you in closing this study are:

What is missing in your family?

What will it take to fill your home with righteousness?

What is your piece of the transformation?

As we come to the end of our study, I hope you have been equipped and encouraged to lead your family to live the life God has for you. Trust Him to do a work in and through you to bring joy, peace and contentment to every member of your family.

May God's peace rest upon you and your family. May His blessing flow over you as you experience the power of His presence in your home. I pray He will guide you and equip you to lead your family successfully.

Appendix One

Answers to Study Questions

Week One
Day One
Matthew 5:1-2

Who is speaking? *Jesus*

Who is the audience? *Disciples and the crowd: two-fold message*

What do you know about the two audiences? *Disciples are close followers of Christ. The crowd may or may not be followers of Christ. Some may merely be curious on-lookers who don't yet know who Jesus is.*

What is the significance of a "two-fold audience"? *Jesus is teaching His disciples how they should live. He is speaking to them based on His assumption that they know Him and His Gospel message. The crowd are simply on-lookers. Jesus isn't necessarily teaching them, but knows that His message will impact some of them. As we live out the impact of the Gospel in our own lives, there are those who are our "disciples." Those who are close to us and experience how we live it out on a daily basis. Then there are onlookers who see us from a distance. Our influence impacts both.*

What is the location of the unfolding story? *On a mountain*

Week One
Day Two
Matthew 5:1-11

Record each of the blessed's/reward for exhibiting that quality.

1. *poor in spirit/kingdom of heaven*
2. *mourn/comforted*

3. *meek/inherit the earth*
4. *hunger and thirst for righteousness/be filled*
5. *merciful/shown mercy*
6. *pure in heart/see God*
7. *peacemakers/called sons of God*
8. *persecuted because of righteousness/theirs is the kingdom of heaven*

Week One
Day Three
Isaiah 61:1-3

Record what Isaiah says about the Lord's favor. *Preach good news to the poor; bind up the brokenhearted; proclaim freedom for the captives; release from darkness for the prisoners; proclaim the Lord's favor; comfort those who mourn; provide for those who grieve; beauty for ashes; gladness for mourning; praise instead of despair.*

Matthew 7:15-20

What is Jesus warning? *Beware of the false prophets.*

What does He say about their ability to deceive? *They come in sheep's clothing but inwardly, they are wolves.*

What do you think Jesus means when He talks about bearing fruit? *He gives an example of how a tree cannot produce any kind of fruit except the kind that is from the inside. Grapes can't come from thorn bushes and figs can't come from thistles.*

Week One
Day Five
John 10:1-18

How does Jesus identify Himself in *John 10:11 & 14*? *I am the Good Shepherd.*

What does the Good Shepherd do for the sheep? *Lays down His life for the sheep; He knows the sheep and the sheep know Him.*

What does *John 10:3-4* say about the Shepherd? *He calls His own sheep by name and leads them out; He goes on ahead of them.*

Week Two
Day One
John 16:17-33

Circle the word "joy" or "rejoices" every time it appears in this passage.

Record everything you learn about the word "joy." *You will weep and mourn while the world rejoices; your grief will turn to joy; forget anguish of childbirth because of the joy of birth; when you see Me again you will rejoice; no one will take away your joy.*

Note the contrasts involving "joy" or "rejoice." *Grief turned to joy; world rejoices while you mourn.*

John 16:33

Why does Jesus say He has "told you these things?" *So that in Him you might find peace.*

What two things does Jesus tell His disciples about the world? *In the world you will have trouble, but Jesus has overcome the world.*

Week Two
Day Four
Philippians 3:13-14

What are the two contrasts Paul makes? *Behind and ahead*

What does he say about these two "times"? *Forget what is behind and strain toward what is ahead.*

What is Paul "pressing on toward"? *The prize for which God has called him heavenward in Christ Jesus.*

Week Three
Day One
2 Corinthians 10:1-7

How does Paul begin this passage? *By the meekness and gentleness of Christ.*

What is the issue that Paul introduces in *2 Corinthians 10:2*? *Some in the church are trying to live by the standards of the world.*

What does Paul tell them in *2 Corinthians 10:3*? *Though we live in the world, we do not wage war as the world does.*

What does he say about the weapons we use to wage war? *Not weapons of the world; have divine power to demolish strongholds.*

Week Three
Day Two
2 Corinthians 12:7-10

What is the reason for Paul's thorn in the flesh? *To keep Paul from becoming conceited because of these surpassingly great revelations.*

What was the thorn? *Messenger of Satan to torment him.*

How many times did Paul ask God to take away the thorn? *Three*

What was God's response? *My grace is sufficient for you, for my power is made perfect in weakness.*

Week Three
Day Three
Matthew 5:43-48

What is the logical worldly advice with regard to enemies? *Hate your enemies.*

What does Jesus say about enemies that is completely counter-culture? *Love your enemies and pray for those who persecute you.*

Week Three
Day Four
2 Chronicles 20:3

What was Jehoshaphat's response to the news that his enemies were after him? *He was alarmed, but the first thing he did was to resolve to inquire of the Lord and proclaim a fast for all of Judah.*

Week Three
Day Five
Psalm 37

Record everything the Psalmist says about the wicked. *Don't fret because of them; like the grass they will soon wither; they will soon die away; don't fret when men succeed in their wicked schemes; they will be cut off; a little while and the wicked will be no more; they will not be found; plot against the righteous; Lord laughs at the wicked; their day is coming; they draw the sword/bend the bow to bring down the poor and needy; slay those whose ways are upright; swords will pierce their own hearts; bows will be broken; power of them will be broken; wicked will perish; they borrow and don't repay; they lie in wait for the righteous, seeking their lives; they will soon pass away and be no more; sinners will be destroyed; future of wicked cut off.*

Now, record everything you are instructed to do in Psalm 37. *Do not fret because of evil men; trust the Lord; do good; dwell in the land; enjoy safe pasture; delight yourself in the Lord; commit your way the Lord; trust in Him; be still before the Lord; wait patiently for Him; do not fret when evil men succeed; refrain from anger; turn away from wrath; do not fret; turn from evil and do good; wait for the Lord; keep His way.*

Record what you learn about those who HOPE in the LORD. *They will inherit the land.*

Record what you learn about the MEEK. *They will inherit the land and enjoy great peace.*

Record what you learn about the BLAMELESS. *Their days are known to the Lord; their inheritance will endure forever; not wither in disaster; in famine they will enjoy plenty.*

Record what you learn about the RIGHTEOUS. *Better the little they have than the wealth of the wicked; the Lord upholds them; they give generously; never forsaken or their children begging bread; always generous and lend freely; their children are blessed; inherit the land and dwell in it forever; mouth utters wisdom; tongue speak with justice; law of God is in his heart; feet do not slip; salvation comes from the Lord; He is their stronghold in time of trouble; Lord help them and delivers them; delivers them from the wicked and saves them because they take refuge in Him.*

What do you learn in *Psalm 37:23? The one in whom the Lord delights: He makes his steps firm; although he stumbles, he won't fall and the Lord upholds him.*

Record what God will do. *IF YOU DELIGHT IN HIM, He will give you the desires of your heart; IF YOU COMMIT YOUR WAY TO THE LORD AND TRUST IN HIM, He will make your righteousness shine like the dawn and the justice or your cause like the noonday sun; laughs at the wicked;*

upholds the righteous; whom the Lord blesses will inherit the land; those He curses will be cut off; loves the just; will not forsake his faithful ones; will protect his faithful ones forever; cut off the offspring of the wicked; He will exalt you to inherit the land; you will see when the wicked are cut off; Lord helps the righteous; delivers the righteous; saves them.

What does *Psalm 37:37* say about the man of peace? *There is a future for him.*

Week Four
Day One
Genesis 17:1-8

How old was Abram when He encountered God in this passage? *99 years old.*

What is God's message to Abram? *God is establishing His covenant to multiply Abram's descendants exceedingly.*

What happens to Abram during this encounter? *His name is changed to Abraham.*

What does God do in Genesis 17:5? *Changes Abram's name to Abraham.*

Week Four
Day Two
John 6:25-35

Record every mention of bread. *You look for me not for miraculous signs but because you ate the loaves. You were filled with what your body craved/needed.*

Jeremiah 23:1-6

What does Jeremiah say about the shepherds that are tending God's flock? *They are destroying and scattering the sheep; they have not attended to the flock.*

Who is going to step in? *God, Himself is going to gather the remnant of the flock from their exile.*

What does Jeremiah 23:5 tell us? *There will come a day when God will raise up a righteous Branch; a king who will reign wisely and do justice in the land; He will save Judah and bring security to Israel.*

What is His name? *The Lord Our Righteousness.*

Week Four
Day Three
John 4:1-26

What does Jesus do in *John 4:7*? *Asks the woman at the well for a drink of water.*

Why do you think He asked her this? *To open a conversation with her.*

What was her response? *Why would you talk to me? She asked this because she was a Samaritan and a woman. In that day, Samaritans were despised by Jews, and a Jewish MAN would never consider talking to a Samaritan woman.*

How did Jesus answer her response? *He piqued her curiosity. He also used an object lesson. They are at a well, drawing physical water to prevent physical thirst. Jesus opens the door of conversation to tell her about the living water that will quench her thirst forever.*

Week Four
Day Four
Deuteronomy 6:4-12

Record anything in this passage that could be considered a command. *Love the Lord your God with all your heart and with all your soul and with all your strength. These commandments that I give you today are to be upon your hearts. Impress them on your children. Talk about them when you sit at home and when you walk along the road, when you lie down and when you get up. Tie them as symbols on your hands and bind them on your forehead. Write them on the doorframes of your houses and on your gates. Be careful that you do not forget the Lord, who brought you out of Egypt, out of the land of slavery.*

Week Five
Day One
Matthew 12:1-8

What did the Pharisees accuse Jesus and His disciples of doing? *Breaking the law by picking grain on the Sabbath.*

What do you think Jesus was trying to say to them with His response? *Basically, their law was all about legalism and had nothing to do with compassion. But compassion is the very heart of God.*

What does Jesus tell them in *Matthew 12:7*? *"I desire mercy, not sacrifice."*

Week Five
Day Four
Matthew 26:69-75

What did Peter do? *He denied that he knew Christ.*

How many times did he do this? *Three times*

When he realized what he had done, what was his response? *He went outside and wept bitterly.*

John 21:15-17

What did Jesus ask Peter? *Peter, do you love me?*

What did Jesus tell Peter to do? *Feed my lambs/sheep*

How many times did Jesus ask the question of Peter? *Three*

Week Five
Day Five
Luke 11:1-13

What was Jesus doing as the passage opens? *Praying*

What did the disciples ask of Jesus? *They wanted Him to teach them how to pray?*

Although scripture doesn't explicitly answer this question, take a minute and consider why you think the disciples would ask Jesus to teach them this one thing? *They observed the power that Jesus had as a result of His prayer life.*

Jesus tells a story in *Luke 11:5*. What do you learn about prayer from the story? *The neighbor responded because of the man's boldness/persistence. God will honor our persistence in prayer.*

Read *Luke 11:9*. What do you learn about prayer? *Jesus teaches that we have to ask, seek and knock in order to receive, find and have the door opened to us.*

Matthew 6:5-14

What is Matthew's warning about prayer? *Don't pray to be seen and applauded by man.*

How does Matthew instruct us to pray? *Go into private and pray to God the Father without having to impress men.*

What is Matthew emphasizing when he warns about babbling? *Don't think God hears your prayers because of the words you use. God already knows what your needs are. He is much more interested in your heart. Do you come before Him with sincerity and trust? Do you believe that He will answer your prayers?*

Week Six
Day One
Psalm 51

Record everything David asks God to do. *Have mercy on me; blot out my transgressions; wash away all my iniquity; cleanse me from my sin; cleanse me with hyssop; wash me; let me hear joy and gladness; let the bones you have crushed rejoice; hide your face from my sins; blot out all my iniquity; create in me a pure heart; renew a steadfast spirit within me; do not cast me from your presence; do not take your Holy Spirit from me; restore to me the joy of your salvation; grant me a willing spirit to sustain me; save me from bloodguilt; open my lips to declare your praise; make Zion prosper; build up the walls of Jerusalem.*

What do you learn from *Psalm 51:6*? *That God desires wisdom and truth on the inside.*

What do you learn from verse *Psalm 51:5*? *Man is sinful from birth; his very nature is sinful.*

What does *Psalm 51:10* say about the heart? *God is the one who gives us a pure heart.*

Week Six
Day Two
Psalm 119:9-11

How can we remain pure? *By living according to God's Word, seeking God with all our heart and hiding God's Word in our heart.*

Week Six
Day Three
Romans 12:1-2

What does Paul tells us to do with our bodies? *Offer them as living sacrifices, holy and pleasing to God.*

What does Paul tell us NOT to do? *Do not conform any longer the pattern of this world.*

What does Paul tell us TO DO? *Be transformed by the renewing of your mind.*

What is the result of the transformation? *You will be able to test and approve what God's will is – His good, pleasing and perfect will.*

Philippians 4:8

Record the list of things that Paul tells us to think about. *True, noble, right, pure, lovely, admirable, excellent, and praiseworthy.*

Week Seven
Day One
Galatians 5:16-25

What was Paul contrasting in *Galatians 5:16-17*? *Spirit versus sinful nature of man.*

What are the acts of the sinful nature Paul records? *Sexual immortality, impurity and debauchery, idolatry and witchcraft, hatred, discord, jealousy, fits of rage, selfish ambition, dissensions factions and envy, drunkenness, orgies, and the like.*

What is the fruit of Spirit Paul notes? *Love, joy, peace, patience, kindness, goodness, faithfulness, gentleness and self-control.*

Psalm 112

Record everything you learn about who man who fears the Lord. *He will have no fear of bad news; his heart is steadfast, trusting in the Lord; his heart is secure; he will have no fear.*

Week Seven
Day Two
Philippians 4:4-7

What does Paul exhort the Philippians to do? *Rejoice always.*

What does Paul say in *Philippians 4:5*? *Let your gentleness be evident to all. The Lord is near.*

In *Philippians 4:6*, what does Paul exhort the Philippians NOT to do? *Be anxious for anything.*

What is his antidote for worry (or being anxious) in the same verse? *Pray.*

What is the result of this in *Philippians 4:7*? *Peace of God, which transcends all understanding will guard your hearts and your minds.*

Week Seven
Day Three
Proverbs 4

Record everything you learn about the instructions of a Father. *Listen to a father's instruction; pay attention and gain understanding; do not forsake my teaching; Lay hold of my words with all your heart; keep my commands and you will live; get wisdom; get understanding; do not forget my words or swerve from them; do not forsake wisdom; get wisdom; get understanding; esteem and embrace understanding; listen and accept what I say; I guide you in the way of wisdom and lead you along straight paths; hold on to instruction, do not let it go; do not set foot on the path of the wicked or walk in the way of evil men; avoid that path and do not travel on it; turn from it and go on your way; he will guide you in the way of wisdom and lead you along straight paths; pay attention to what I say; listen closely to my words; do not let them out of your sight; keep them within your heart; guard your heart above all else; put away perversity from your mouth; keep corrupt talk far from your lips; let your eyes look straight ahead; fix your gaze directly before you; make level paths for your feet; take only ways that are firm; do not swerve to the right or left; keep your foot from evil.*

Record all the benefits to the son. *You will live; wisdom will protect you and watch over you; understanding will exalt and honor you; the years of your life will be many; straight paths, steps not hampered; won't stumble; instruction is your life; father's words are life and health.*

Record everything you learn about wisdom in the passage. *Get it; Do not forsake it and you will be protected; love it and you will be watched over; wisdom is supreme, therefore get it; father will guide you in the ways of wisdom.*

Week Seven
Day Four
Ephesians 4:17-5:2

What is the contrast Paul draws between the Gentiles and the Ephesian believers? *Gentiles: futility of thinking/darkened in their understanding/separated from the life of God because of the ignorance that is in them due to the hardening of their hearts. Ephesian believers: Heard of Christ and were taught in him in accordance with the truth that is in Jesus.*

What does Paul tell the Ephesian church to "put on" and "take off"? *Take off old self which is being corrupted by its deceitful desires/falsehood. Put on the new self in the attitude of your minds/created to be like God in true righteousness and holiness.*

What does Paul say about anger? *In your anger do not sin; do not let the sun go down on your anger and give the devil a foothold.*

What does he say about stealing? *Don't steal. Instead, work by doing something useful with your own hands to share with those in need.*

What does Paul warn about talk? *Do not let any unwholesome talk come out of your mouth but only what is helpful for building others up according to their needs, benefitting those who listen.*

What are we to get rid of? *Bitterness, rage and anger, brawling and slander, every form of malice.*

What are we to do instead? *Be kind and compassionate to each other. Forgive each other just as Christ forgave us. Imitate God as dearly loved children. Live a life of love, just as Christ loved us.*

Week Seven
Day Five
Psalm 16:5-11

Who has assigned the boundaries? *The Lord*

Where have the boundary lines fallen? *In pleasant places*

How does David respond to the boundaries? *Praise the Lord who counsels him*

What is the result of the boundaries? *David's heart is glad, His tongue rejoices and his body will rest secure, he will not be abandoned to the grave nor will the Holy One (Christ) see decay. This is a reference to the fact that Christ, although dead and in the tomb, will be resurrected before there is the decay of death.*

What does God do in *Psalm 16:11*? *Make known the path of life; fill with joy in God's presence, fill with eternal pleasures.*

Week Eight
Day One
Job 1:1-5

Record everything you learn about Job. *He was blameless, upright, feared God and shunned evil; had 7 sons and 3 daughters; he owned 7,000 sheep, 3,000 camels, 500 yoke of oxen and 500 donkeys; he had a large number of servants; greatest man in the East; he would sacrifice an offering for his children in case they had sinned and cursed God in their hearts.*

Job 1:6-12

Whose idea was it for Satan to "touch" Job's life? *God's idea*

What did Satan say to God in *Job 1:9*? *He questioned Job's sincerity. Since God had put a hedge of protection around Job, why wouldn't he live righteously?*

Job 1:13-19

What did Satan take from Job? *Oxen, donkeys, servants, sheep, servants, camels, servants, sons and daughters.*

Job 1:20-22

What was Job's response to the news? *He got up and tore his robe and shaved his head. Then he fell to the ground in worship.*

Record what Job says in *Job 1:21. Naked I came from my mother's womb, and naked I will depart. The Lord gave and the Lord has taken away; may the name of the Lord be praised.*

Write out *Job 1:22. In all this, Job did not sin by charging God with wrongdoing.*

Week Eight
Day Two
Job 2:1-10

What else does God allow Satan to do to Job? *Afflict him physically, but could not take his life.*

What does Job's wife have to say? *Curse God so that you can just die.*

How does Job reply? *You are talking like a foolish woman. Shall we accept good from God, and not trouble?*

Week Eight
Day Four
Hebrews 12:1-2

What are we to "throw off"? *Everything that hinders and the sin that so easily entangles.*

How are we to run? *With perseverance.*

Appendix Two

Suggestions for Small Group Discussion

Welcome to the study of the *BE-Attitudes for Blending Families*. I hope your group will enjoy sharing this eight week journey together. As we join Jesus on the mountain, let's consider the power available to you as you study together. Each week I hope everyone in the group is able to prioritize spending time in the study of God's Word. As a Bible teacher, I cannot emphasize enough the power you will experience in your life when you make spending time with God the most important time of the day. Allow God to speak to your heart as you pray and open His Word.

To the Group Facilitator: Praying for those in your group is the most important thing you can do. Consider developing a method for keeping record of prayer requests throughout the study. Sometimes talking about prayer requests can take up a large portion of your class time. Be aware that listing requests is not praying. Here is a suggestion for keeping the prayer time about praying instead of talking. You may want to provide index cards for people to write down requests. That way, you just pick up the cards and get straight to praying. You might want to distribute the cards around the room and allow different people to voice the prayers. This will keep the prayer time focused on prayer, but will also provide written records of what your group has prayed for.

Encourage your group to share what God has taught them during their study throughout the week. It is always a good idea to create a "safe" environment in which to share. Some of the topics and discussions may be sensitive. Remind group members that in order for this to remain a safe place to share, they need to keep the discussions "within the room." Our human nature tempts us to share other people's private issues with others. You are not coming together to gather information on others in the group. You are coming together to grow in the Lord, and encourage each other along life's journey.

The discussion points provided in this section are merely suggestions. Please feel free to use your own questions and discussion starters. Allow the inspiration of the Holy Spirit to lead the group. Allow time for the group to share with each other. The first few weeks will likely be a time of building relationships. But as the weeks progress, the level of comfort will help with sharing and discussion. While personal examples can be helpful, do your best to keep the discussion focused on the week's lesson topic and scripture passages. This is not a counseling group, it is a Bible study group.

I hope your group will find this study helpful in managing [re]marriages and blending families. Remember the power of prayer as you lead. Pray for your group members and their families. Pray for yourself and your own family that God would use you as a vessel of healing and hope.

I am praying for you as you lead. Allow God to use your gifts and your experiences to strengthen you as you lead. Trust God for wisdom and guidance, and know that the Holy Spirit can and will do a work through your leadership in the group.

Week One

Blessed are the poor in spirit, for theirs is the kingdom of heaven. Matthew 5:3

This week's study lays the groundwork for Jesus' Sermon on the Mount.

- Encourage the group to share any observations they had as they read through and began to process the beatitudes in *Matthew 5:1-11*.
- Days four and five of this week's lesson focus on the first beatitude. Allow opportunity for group members to share any insights they gained regarding what it means to be poor in spirit.
- Encourage group members to discuss the foundation of their new family. As this beatitude lays the foundation for living victoriously, what have they done or can they do as a family to build a strong foundation?
- Discuss what they learned about dependence.
- Discuss *John 10:1-18*. Use the questions from the lesson to guide your discussion.

The foundation for life is having a relationship with Jesus Christ as Savior. Be sensitive to anyone who may have family members who have not yet accepted Christ's gift of salvation. Commit to pray for anyone in the group who is not yet a believer.

Notes:

Week Two

Blessed are those who mourn, for they will be comforted. Matthew 5:4

Mourning is a painful experience, yet everyone in your group has walked the journey. They have all lost something in order to gain their new family.

- Discuss *John 16:17-33*. What did group members learn from the passage? Was there a particularly meaningful insight anyone gained?
- Discuss the stages of grief. You need only focus on stages that are relevant to the group. Allow time for discussion.
- Spend time in prayer. Pray specifically for any group members or family members who are still struggling through grief.
- Allow members to discuss any ideas or insights they have which might help others as they deal with grief.
- At the end of day five, a list of suggestions was provided to help people through their grief. Allow time for group members to share other ideas that may have been helpful to them or someone in their family as they journeyed through the stages of grief.

The study this week may have been difficult for some in the group. Be particularly attentive to anyone who may need special prayer this week.

Notes:

Week Three

Blessed are the meek, for they will inherit the earth. Matthew 5:5

Our topic for the week focused primarily on relationships with an ex-spouse. While this may be one of the most difficult relationships in a blending family, it can also be one of victory when we allow the Holy Spirit to do a work in us and through us. Be careful during this week's discussion that it not become an opportunity to complain about ex-spouses. The purpose of the study is to equip us to be overcomers in how we live out our relationship with Christ. Be on guard if the discussion becomes unwholesome or unkind. You may want to open the discussion by reading *Ephesians 4:29-5:2.*

> *Do not let any unwholesome talk come out of your mouths, but only what is helpful for building others up according to their needs, that it may benefit those who listen. And do not grieve the Holy Spirit of God, with whom you were sealed for the day of redemption. Get rid of all bitterness, rage and anger, brawling and slander, along with every form of malice. Be kind and compassionate to one another, forgiving each other, just as in Christ God forgave you. Be imitators of God, therefore as dearly loved children and live a life of love, just as Christ loved us and gave himself up for us as a fragrant offering and sacrifice to God.*

- Discuss the meaning of meekness.
- Encourage group members to share any insights they gained from *2 Corinthians 10:4-5.*
- Discuss what group members learned about Paul's thorn in the flesh and how they can apply the principle to life with an ex-spouse.
- Discuss *Matthew 5:43-48.* Allow group members to share any insights they gained regarding building a more positive relationship with an ex-spouse.
- Discuss what you learned from Jehoshaphat about doing battle.
- Using the questions in the lesson, discuss *Psalm 37.*

Spend time praying for each other as you close your time together. Pray specifically for ex-spouse relationships. Remind group members that the goal is to be healthy as a blending family. Until there is some resolution in the relationship with an ex-spouse, there will be turmoil in the blending family. Pray for honest communication in the blending family regarding issues with ex-spouses. Pray against the comparison game when it comes to whose ex is harder to deal with. As much as it depends on you, be at peace with everyone.

Notes:

Week Four

Blessed are those who hunger and thirst for righteousness, for they will be filled. Matthew 5:6

This week's beatitude relates to step-parenting. As with last week's discussion of ex-spouses, be careful that this week does not become a gripe session about the children. While frustrations are very real and not at all unusual, the purpose of the discussion is to bring help and hope as we parent someone else's children. You might have the group consider how they would feel if their children were together in a group and all they did was complain about their parents. Be careful about how you allow the discussion to progress.

- How did learning about El-Shaddai help you to trust God to take care of you and your family?
- Allow group members to discuss some of the most pressing issues regarding step-parenting.
- Discuss what it means to step-parent righteously.
- Discuss *Psalm 107.* Allow group members to share how they might apply the THRIVE acrostic to their family situation.
- Allow time for group members to share positive ideas and insights they have gained as step-parents.

Close your time together by praying for each other's children. Especially pray for positive relationships to develop and grow between step-parents and stepchildren. Encourage the group to pray for each other throughout the week.

Notes:

Week Five

Blessed are the merciful, for they will be shown mercy. Matthew 5:7

This week we studied forgiveness and trust. Give group members a chance to discuss any questions or problems they encounter as they choose to forgive. Discuss any difficulties they experience.

- Discuss the difference between grace and mercy.
- Discuss what forgiveness is NOT.
- Allow group members to discuss Matthew *18:21-35*. Did anyone gain any new insights from this passage?
- Discuss what you learned about forgiveness from day three.
- Discuss *Genesis 50:15-21*. Ask group members to share any application they made from this passage.
- Ask group members to discuss any examples or experiences they have had regarding forgiveness as discussed on day three.
- Discuss the relationship between forgiveness and trust.
- At the end of this week's lesson, a family activity was suggested. Give group members an opportunity to share any activities they have done to strengthen their family bond.

Pray for group members to be forgiving. Pray for any specific relationships that need forgiveness.

Notes:

Week Six

Blessed are the pure in heart, for they will see God. Matthew 5:8

- Discuss *Psalm 51*. Ask group members to share their insights.
- Discuss *Psalm 119:9-11*. How does this passage help us understand how to maintain a pure heart?
- Discuss *Romans 12:-1-2*. Use the questions in the lesson for discussion.
- Ask group members to share their word lists from *Philippians 4:8*.
- Allow group members to share about their family's transformation process.

Close the group session by praying for each family represented. Pray for God's purity to rule their homes. Pray for pure hearts.

Notes:

Week Seven

Blessed are the peacemakers for they will be called sons of God. Matthew 5:9

Allow group members to share any struggles they may have regarding stepsiblings. Have them share any insights gained from the lesson for day one.

- Discuss *Philippians 4:4-7*.
- Discuss what you learned about discipline from *Proverbs 4*.
- Discuss what you learned about parenting as a team.
- Discuss what you learned about communication from *Ephesians 4:17-5:2*.
- How can you apply *Psalm 16:5-6* to setting boundaries for your family? Ask group members to share how they set boundaries in their home and family. What works well? What hasn't worked so well?

Allow time for group members to share practical suggestions they may have on any of the topics covered this week. Close in prayer.

Notes:

Week Eight

Blessed are those who are persecuted because of righteousness, for theirs is the kingdom of heaven. Matthew 5:10.

This week, we need to be careful about considering ourselves persecuted. While we may encounter some criticism, or may be treated unfairly because of our faith, we really cannot consider those injustices in the same vain as persecution the way many of our brothers and sisters around the world are suffering. There are Christians around the world who are tortured and executed because of their faith. We certainly cannot put our feelings of being treated unfairly in the same camp. However, we do have an understanding of enduring difficulties and struggles when we seemingly have done nothing to deserve injustice.

- What did you take away from the discussion of Job's life experiences? How can that shape your perspective when you encounter difficult circumstances?
- Discuss *Hebrews 12:1-2*. Encourage group members to share how they have applied this to their personal life and blending family.
- Allow time for group members to share about their experience in the passages about experiencing joy in life.

As you close the session, be intentional about providing opportunity for group members to remain connected. Hopefully everyone has walked away with a deeper value for living life in community. Perhaps you will plan another study to do together. Close in prayer.

Notes:

Endnotes

[1]   Ross, Allen. The Beatitudes (Matthew 5:1-12), March 2006, Bible.org

[2]   Dictionary.reference.com

[3]   Tuckman, Bruce (1965). "Developmental sequence in small groups". *Psychological Bulletin* **63** (6): 384–99.

[4]   From the results of a ChristiaNet poll reported by Marketwire.com.

[5]   Spurgeon, Charles H. "Psalm 112:1," The Treasury of David. Biblestudytools.org.

[6]   Trust His Heart. Words and Music by Eddie Carswell and Babbie Mason. Recorded by Babbie Mason. Copyright 1989, Dayspring Music, LLC.